ÂF451187

www.elveaverlag.de
Contact: elvea@t-online.de

© ELVEA 2024

All rights reserved.
The work may be used, even in part,
only with the permission of the publisher be passed on.

Author: Antje Haugg

Editing: Maite Schmidt / Sabrina Haugg / Heather Ritter

Translated with a foreword by Chris Ritter

Cover Design/Graphics: ELVEA

Layout: Uwe Köhl

ISBN: 978-3-946751-30-4

Antje Haugg

A Very Musical Murder

A little background …

by Chris Ritter

Bayreuth Festival Theatre

A Very Musical Murder, original German title *Notenspur in Moll*, had as its genesis a project undertaken by an extra-curricular class to celebrate the 150th anniversary in 2017 of Richard Wagner Gymnasium, an academic high school in Bayreuth, Germany.

Bayreuth is a small Bavarian town in the very heart of Europe, 235 kilometres north of Munich, the state capital. The modern state of Bavaria is divided politically into seven administrative regions which reflect the historical, cultural and linguistic diversity of the German lands that were amalgamated into what is now the *Free State of Bavaria* in the nineteenth century. The identity of only three of these administrative regions (*Upper Bavaria, Lower Bavaria* and *Upper Palatinate*) is truly Bavarian. Three other administrative regions have quite another identity altogether, stemming from the historical region of Franconia (*Upper*, *Middle* and *Lower Franconia*). Bayreuth is the capital of one of these three administrative regions, Upper Franconia. Franconia as a whole is quite distinct culturally and linguistically from historical Bavaria.

In *A Very Musical Murder*, it soon becomes clear that Franconians, represented by the citizens of Bayreuth, consider themselves as very different in every respect from the Bavarians to their south and east.

The Free State of Bavaria

Internationally, Bayreuth's claim to fame comes from quite another quarter. For lovers of classical music, the names Richard Wagner and Bayreuth are synonymous. Every year in August the Bayreuth Music Festival, featuring Wagner's Ring Cycle of operas, is staged at Wagner's purpose-built Festival Theatre on Green Hill. Wagner lovers come from all over the world to pay homage to the composer and his music at what is one of the highlights of the world classical music calendar.

Why such an important event is staged far from the main German cultural centres in the big cities goes back to Wagner wanting to establish financial independence and control over the production of his works. In Bayreuth he could present and benefit from his own productions, have full copyright control of his works and enjoy total cultural dominance. Wagner was also attracted to Bayreuth because it already possessed a splendid theatre for staging opera, the Margravial Opera House (*Markgräfliches Opernhaus*), a baroque wonder that is now on the UNESCO World Heritage List.

Unfortunately for Wagner, this opera house proved inadequate for large scale productions. Undeterred, he then went about building his very own theatre in the north of Bayreuth.

The first concert in Wagner's new Festival Theatre was held in 1876, nine years after the founding of the 'Higher Girls' School' that would become the now co-educational school that bears his name, Richard Wagner Gymnasium.

A Very Musical Murder was originally conceived as a play by the school drama coordinator, Angelika Guder-Späth. The extracurricular class went under the rubric 'Crime Scene Bayreuth – Hunt for Clues at RWG', so Angelika Guder-Späth came up with the idea of presenting the play as a murder mystery that linked the school's 150th anniversary with its 50th anniversary in 1917 during the darkest days of the First World War.

Antje Haugg, as a celebrated local author of crime novels, was enlisted to contribute to the text of the play. As she notes in her conclusion, 'it soon became clear that it would not remain just a murder mystery that was going to be staged as a play in the anniversary year, but that a book of the play was also going to appear'.

In this way, *A Very Musical Murder* evolved from a play into this novel.

A few sentences beforehand …

Even if some characters who appear in this novel, like Katharina Wagner or the Kremnitz couple, are not fictitious, but actually live in Bayreuth or Emtmannsberg, I would nevertheless like to stress that this murder mystery is a complete fiction, so that all the events depicted here have no connection with real events.

As far as I know, there has never been a Zweistein Sonata. All the legends and myths that are entwined with this piece are similarly products of the author's imagination, as is the whole Zweistein family and Albert's connection with Siegfried Wagner.

Equally fictitious are all the rumours about the involvement of our characters in the fire at the Crystal Spa and the alienation of new construction sites round about Bayreuth.

I would like to make excuses beforehand to all those readers of the German edition who are disappointed that I do not have Lotte Kerner speaking exclusively in Bayreuth dialect. But in consideration of all readers who do not come from Franconia, it seemed advisable to keep with a language that is easy to read – with a few notable exceptions.

Finally – of course, I know that the beer festival normally takes place in August. Unfortunately, this date had to be moved to fit in with the rest of the plot.

Antje Haugg

1

Prologue

The girl sat at the piano, fully absorbed in her playing. She plunged herself into the music, becoming one with the sonata whose resounding chords filled the room with mystical life. She could already play long passages by heart, only now and then needing to glance up at the score. The melody, its composer soon to be described by the critics as 'more brilliant than Liszt and Wagner – a new star risen in the firmament of Bayreuth music', rang out just for her. She was not going to allow any listener to enjoy the rich, brimming chords, allow any teacher to eavesdrop, fascinated by her student's performance. No, she was playing only for herself. Tears ran down her face, tears of hot, melancholy sorrow for her father. He had entrusted and bequeathed this music to her. This music was his legacy.

Distracted by a fleeting shadow, she glanced across to the ground-level basement window. For a moment that magically stretched out forever, she gazed directly into steel-blue eyes that appeared ready to gobble her up, but at the same time threatened to drown her. Then the spell broke and she gave a start, as did the man at the window. The face vanished as suddenly as it had appeared.

Her heart pounded, terror gripped her, and the words of her mother rang in her ears as if the quarrel between her parents had been just yesterday: "Your damned music will be the ruin of all of us!"

Confused and frightened, she anxiously shuffled the sheets of music into a disorderly pile, pressed them to her chest and stood up. It would be best to go, right away.

Again, a shadow, now at the window right at the back of the room. *He has come over here. He has run right round the building.*

Panic-stricken, she turned and rushed out of the music room. The only door to the outside world would lead her directly into his arms. She looked round desperately – the coal cellar. She ran to her left, through the open cellar door, quickly and softly shutting it behind her. The long, dark corridor stretched before her. To the left the coal cellar branched off, but that only took her attention for an instant. Straight ahead stood the heavy old wooden door. She knew it could be bolted from the inside. Trembling she ran up to it and slipped through to the other, safer side. Nervously, she felt for the bolt in the semi-darkness and pushed it across. She let go, relieved, but the door softly creaked open again a few centimetres. Now that her eyes had adjusted to the dark, she could see why: the bolt hole had sheared away from the wall and was unable to hold the door, the plaster having crumbled away. Without reflecting, she hurried on, further and further, until bashing, face first, into a cold wall. Shaking her throbbing head, she looked round and recognised where she was. The way she was going went only a few metres further and then through a door up into the school building. She did not look for a key, knowing no key had ever been hidden there. For a moment she listened intently to make out if he had followed her. Not hearing anything, she calmed herself down a bit and took a moment to collect her thoughts.

Having composed herself, she now scampered silently up the cold stone steps and wooden staircase to the attic. She could hide herself there, she would be safe there …

She did not doze off in her hiding place wedged between old pieces of furniture and curtains. At most it was only exhaustion she felt, from having to wait so long. It would soon be dark outside. At some stage she would be looked for, of that she was certain. And then she would be out of danger.

Soft creaking brought back her panic. She held her breath, praying desperately to have imagined the eerie sound. In vain – a new creak on the wooden staircase. He was coming up. He knew she was there. They would all be ruined.

One other possibility remained – the tower. With the sheets of music once more pressed tightly to her chest, she scurried to the door. Behind it a steep narrow steel ladder led up to the clock tower. Wildly determined, she clambered up it – he would not find the door, he would not find the ladder – he would simply not think there was a tower there.

She was wrong.

He spoke in a completely normal, soft voice, but every word sent shivers down her spine.

"Margarethe, come down to me. I'll take you home. And first you can play me that beautiful piece that I could hear from outside. Now, come on, dear. You know me. Look, it's already dark. People will talk if you're not home soon. Surely you don't want any gossip. Doesn't your poor mother have enough worries? Come on, I'll take you safely home."

She looked round, eyes wide with terror – she was caught in a trap. There was no way out.

Really no way? The tilt window. She was small and delicate for her age; she could squeeze through it and climb onto the roof. He would not be able to follow her through – he was too big.

The extremity of her situation had made her forget her fear of heights. Normally she stepped back in fright when she looked out of a window on the second floor. Not now. With scrabbling fingers, she pushed the handle up, forced the window open and slipped out headfirst.

She screamed loudly when she felt the hard grip around her ankle. She had been too slow. He had reeled her in. He would pull her back into the tower and then …

Again, she was wrong. But the time between the hefty push and the hard landing on the paved schoolyard did not really last long enough for her to realise her error.

She lay dying in the darkness.

Some of the pages of music flapped around haphazardly, until he came, with his steel-blue eyes, and collected them. He had to pull the last sheet forcibly out of her hand, a sheet she had grabbed convulsively in her death throes.

"Why didn't you listen to me? Outside in the dark is no place for girls your age. You know that. You should have let me take you home. Really."

Again, that tone of voice, this time seeping into her consciousness through a swelling roar in her head.

He observed her with interest, how the thin trickles of blood running out of her nose joined the thicker dribbles coming out of the corner of her mouth. He examined the twitching eyelids, the eyeballs still rolling underneath, so only the whites were visible, and the twisted body parts, the numerous broken bones, all joining to form a grotesque artwork.

At the end, her gaze cleared for a short moment – she stared at him, accusingly, full of pain, full of incomprehension. She plunged into his steel-blue eyes.

And passed away.

2

Autumn, 2017

"Oh my God – what was I thinking?"

Doris Lech was staring at the *North Bavaria Courier* that lay spread out before her on the kitchen table. She was filled with a strange mixture of disbelief and frustration and finally slapped the open, double-sided spread of the 'What's On' section with the flat of her hand. What was grinning at her in freshly printed black and white was an impertinence, at least in Doris' eyes. It was – simply, nothing: St Michael's Fair in Weidenberg; tattoo expo in Bindlach; Bayreuth Autumn Motor Show in the pedestrian zone; a children's concert by the Sparrow Choir; on Sunday, a guided tour through the Ecological Botanical Garden under the title 'Autumn in the EBG'; a presumably more than amateurish theatre production by the 'Stage Sprinters', a minor sporting club, with the title 'Falling Leaves, Falling Bodies'; on Saturday from 7:00 am to 1:00 pm, the Bayreuth weekly market in the renovated Red Main Hall; and, in the Red Main Centre, a special exhibition with the motto 'our youngest explore with finger paints'.

Nothing, but absolutely nothing of all the things that had spontaneously occurred to Doris when she read, half a year ago, the fateful job advertisement: *Bayreuth – Wagner, Liszt: pure music heaven, where you can hear beautiful music wherever you turn.* That is what she had thought. Pure culture.

She wrote her application listening to Lohengrin, without hesitating for a moment, without doing any research; and they had hired her.

Had she burned all her bridges without batting an eyelid? Cologne – it was in the past. For long enough, she had been passed over for promotions. For long enough, she had been punished with a lack of respect from her employers. For long enough, she had been looked at sideways by her workmates. To be precise, she had been side-lined ever since she had poked around too deeply in the hornet's nest of the building authority.

Perhaps she should have listened to her boss at the time, when he told her, "Frau Lech, simply let it be. There are things that shouldn't be stirred up, both for the good of the public and for your own sake."

At the time she had had a blazing argument with him about what constituted 'the good of the public' and about her responsibility for that good. And she had begun to stir up things that he wanted left undisturbed.

She had not got far. There were people who had the whip hand and let her know it, showing no mercy. And from then on, she no longer had any prospects in Cologne.

Bayreuth – it sounded like the ultimate paradise to the lover of Wagnerian Opera. And that is why she had applied for the job without researching, without finding out more, totally untypical of her. Doris Lech was famous as the cool thinker, the clear-sighted, logical investigator. *That* Doris would have found out beforehand what went on in Bayreuth after the last curtain of the season had dropped in Wagner's Opera House on Green Hill, in the next eleven months when the words 'world city' had no meaning there.

In short – her relocation at the beginning of September happened at possibly the most inauspicious time. Wagner had had his day for that year. Everyone seemed, above all, to want to recover from the overdose of culture of the previous four weeks. The excited chatter of the Festival Youth Club volunteers that had filled the pedestrian zone in the summer had fallen silent. Nothing remained of the international flair that came down from Green Hill and lay over the town like a colourful veil every August. The temporary walkways were folded back up and the city of culture had fallen back into its Sleeping Beauty stupor.

Doris Lech would have liked to have howled with rage. This page with its wretched 'What's On' notices made it clear to her how stupid she had been. Her boss had been right, even then, when he had labelled her naïve, inexperienced in the ways of the world. It was as if he had already guessed what sort of idiocy she would again let herself be carried away by. What on earth had she been thinking?

Furious, she grabbed the coffee cup and took a hasty gulp. It burned her tongue straight away, which seemed to her a fitting reminder of her screwed up life.

In a headlong rush she had given everything up: her job, which even without the prospect of promotion was at least secure; the spacious apartment in her parents' city villa with a view over the Rhine; her friendship group; her relationship; and the precious variety of things to do and see in a city like Cologne.

Doris breathed deeply, leafed through the *Courier* and drank another mouthful of coffee, this time with more care and awareness.

No, it had been the right decision. She had only to consider her situation now and keep that in the front of her mind. If she was honest – and that was easier if she did not have the 'What's On' section of the paper staring her in the face – then she had to admit that her old job had become more than awful in the last few years. The really interesting cases had no longer been given to her but to workmates. Of course, she was still a detective chief superintendent, but her most recent work reviews had been altogether negative, having, as she was well aware, nothing to do with her work but everything to do with her having dug once more into matters that were none of her business, at least in the opinion of her boss.

The apartment had in reality been far too big for her alone, a fact that the superb view over the Rhine could not hide. Peter had only ever half-heartedly thought of moving in. Actually, he had never thought of a serious relationship at all, and she had simply not wanted to admit it. Now she was thirty-seven years old and had waited for seven years on an offer of marriage that had never come. Peter had not even wanted an apartment together. And that too was certainly, at least partially, due to what had not been said. It would have looked bad for a star architect to appear with a partner who had given the building authority a hard time. Occasional nights together was all the relationship had ever extended to. There had been no more feeling of 'us' than that.

As for her family, her parents, whatever their true thoughts, had always only made mildly veiled reproaches. Firstly, about her dropping out of her architecture course and instead joining the Criminal Investigation Branch. Doris Lech, daughter of a well-known building contractor in the city, Cologne old money – how could she? And then, how had she not managed to hold onto Peter? If she had, that would have made up for everything as far as her parents were concerned. A prominent name, a successful son-in-law – but it was not to be. Narrowly connected to this was the question of children. Doris was the only daughter, the whole hope of the family. She should have borne children to extend the family name into the distant, unknown future. And what had she done? Simply nothing. Which at the time had really not been her fault. There had been a time when Doris would have preferred nothing better than to have started a family with Peter. He was the one who had put a stop to that. Perhaps she should have dumped him earlier and looked for someone else. But how, when her heart did not play along?

Oh, and going out to concerts. She should not have gone to them so often that they mattered. If she was completely honest with herself, it had rather bored and annoyed her to constantly see the same faces at the same concerts, and she had always been branded an outsider. Moreover, her friendship circle had shrunk drastically in the last years. She was no rebel; she was simply someone who had fouled her nest in the eyes of many of her acquaintances.

No, it had really been the right decision to turn her back on Cologne. The meagre events program on offer in the *North Bavaria Courier* did not change that. Things would change. Her assistant, Lotte Kerner, had listed some events that she could look forward to: Jazz November, concerts in the Reichshof Culture Stage, the Easter Festival, the Studio Stage. Even if, due to renovations, the City Hall Theatre would be shut as a performance space for the foreseeable future, a few interesting productions were nevertheless waiting for Doris at other venues. Just not today or tomorrow, a consolation that nevertheless left a rather stale aftertaste.

Doris stared out through the small kitchen window. There was not much to see in the foggy grey of early Saturday morning. The weekend would not have much more to offer, there was no changing that. She drank a last gulp of her now lukewarm, equally stale tasting coffee, folded up her newspaper and seriously considered paying her landlady a visit. Perhaps Frau König would have a useful suggestion regarding weekend activities. And since she lived in the same building, it would be no world trip going to see her. On the other hand – with two children, the ten-year-old Jonas and Lena, six years older and deep in the throes of puberty, Frau König would presumably have a completely different idea of successful leisure activities to her.

What else? With a gentle sigh, she grabbed her phone and wrote a message to Lotte, in the certain conviction that Lotte would not answer before half past eleven, as it was guaranteed she would have been out very late the night before.

But first there was the weekly market to visit. She made herself presentable for a trip into town and set off. The early bird still got its worm there. So she managed to snare a loaf of the sought after Buchauer wood oven bread and a pound of the intensively tasty self-grown Campari tomatoes from the Gräbner market garden. Late-sleepers like Lotte missed out on such pleasures.

In a somewhat better mood, and with her purchases in her wicker basket, Doris strolled through the Red Main Centre and looked for a new coat. The sad colour offering of the new collections was altogether suited to make her depressed. She finally discovered a mouse-grey short coat that was at least well-cut, and, after a brief reflection, bought it.

She then cast an eye over the considerably more colourful art exhibition. The works of the little artists were actually for sale. Irritated, Doris looked more closely. Yes, the pictures could be purchased, proceeds going to the Immenreuth SOS Children's Village. Presumably, parents and grandparents made up ninety percent of the investors in the project. A new wave of melancholy overcame Doris, combined with a bad conscience about having almost passed by without paying the least attention. She examined what was on offer picture by picture. She had just paid almost €200 for a coat – why, exactly? Only because her old coat was already three years old? She stared at her shopping bag, then she impulsively turned round and took the coat back to the shop. A short time later she again stood in front of the pictures. After a short hesitation she decided on a work by little Miriam that could have depicted an exploding floral meadow or perhaps daytime fireworks – it did not have a title and therefore left plenty of room for interpretation. The coat money found its way into the till of the children's village and Doris wedged the artwork under her arm. Back home, she took down the Spitzweg print that in Frau König's opinion perfectly rounded off the furnished apartment, instead, hanging up the new purchase, writing on a big white sticker 'The End of the World in E Flat Major' and sticking it on the bottom right corner. Grinning with satisfaction, she stepped back and examined the work. Perfect! That was exactly the amount of sarcasm which suited her mood.

She made herself yet another coffee, buttered two pieces of her Buchauer bread with butter also bought at the weekly market, cut up three tomatoes and sprinkled them with salt. Indeed, Bayreuth did have its good sides, even away from Festival Hill. Doris fished her phone out of her jacket pocket and checked if Lotte had already answered. Her assistant had, in fact, woken up in the meantime and had sent the ultimate event tip: *Plant market in Emtmannsberg today from 2:00 pm – coffee and cakes, plant exchange and definitively the world's best banana Swiss roll. I'll be there in any case.*

The chief inspector stared at the message. She would not have minded if Lotte was joking. But then she thought, no, it was a serious suggestion. Lotte would truly be there and would eagerly join in. Two weeks ago, she had gone to the Emtmannsberg Garlic Festival at the insistent urging of her assistant and Lotte had rushed around in the centre of the action. She had enthusiastically helped out, had made Doris known to half of Emtmannsberg, and had stacked Doris' plate with a selection of what she had to admit were very tasty garlic specialities.

Plant market? Actually, why not? Perhaps there would be indoor plants there; her apartment was terribly bare and could do with a little green. And with luck the sun might come out later and then the 20° mark might be reached one more time for the year – at least Nina Blindzellner, the announcer on the local radio station, Radio Main, was convinced it would.

She searched for an outfit that in her opinion suited a plant market and put on jeans, a polo shirt and her light brown leather jacket. She did not possess garden shoes, so she decided after a brief period of hesitation for light brown short boots, whose heels were guaranteed to remain inconspicuous in any garden.

Her secret quirk, to want to appear taller than she actually was by wearing high heels, would be rather counterproductive today. After all, the 1.67 metre Doris had effortlessly met the selection criteria of the State Police. But the years with Peter had shaped her – next to the handsome giant she had never really stood out – something the high heels had done little to change. She stared thoughtfully at her shoe cupboard – not one pair of trainers fit for street wear. Something else she ought to change. But that would have to wait till next Saturday …

3

Doris Lech looked frantically but in vain for an old carton or even a collapsible box that she could stick indoor plants in – provided, of course, she could find anything at all for her apartment at the plant exchange.

She had driven the winding stretch to Emtmannsberg just recently and knew one thing for sure, she didn't want to subject her car or the flowerpots to constant rolling around. Not that in any case she could fit many into her red BMW convertible. With a frustrated sigh, she gave up the search and decided instead to ask her landlady, Frau König, if she had a box she could lend her. Shortly after, she climbed up the extra floor to her landlady's apartment and rang the bell. She heard quick pattering steps, then Jonas tore the door open with so much force that the door handle banged against the wall. A loud and reproachful 'Jonas' rang out from the kitchen, without, however, having any obvious effect on the boy.

"Mum, Frau Lech is here," he yelled, then left Doris standing and whizzed back into his bedroom. Frau König came out of the kitchen shaking her head and spoke to Doris in her thick Franconian dialect.

"Hello, Frau Lech. I'm sorry, Jonas is like that. He's just got back from visiting his godfather, who wants to take him to the movies. That's why he's so excited. Come in."

Doris followed her landlady into the kitchen and sat on the chair that Frau König pushed towards her. On the table lay greens for soup and a variety of vegetables: potatoes, a kohlrabi, a few small zucchinis. Frau König grabbed a knife and turned her attention back to preparing the midday meal. For a short, melancholy moment Doris compared her landlady's life with her own. They were about the same age; it could be Doris and not Frau König preparing a meal for her family. She forcefully pushed this thought aside as Frau König spoke to her.

"What is it then, is there something wrong with your apartment?"

Doris brushed this suggestion aside.

"No, everything is excellent. It's just that I'd like to drive to Emtmannsberg. There's a plant exchange there today, and perhaps I might find a few indoor plants. But I don't have a box to put the pots in and I don't want to get dirt everywhere. That's why I wanted to ask if perhaps you might have a carton or a collapsible box that I can borrow?"

Frau König paused for a moment and lay the knife back on the table.

"Why, of course. But wait a minute – Emtmannsberg? I want to go there myself. I need a few things for my garden. Wouldn't you rather go with us?"

That was naturally a sensible idea. Doris privately said goodbye to the essentially not sensible idea of travelling to Emtmannsberg in radiant sunshine with the roof of her convertible down. Two hours later she and Frau König climbed into the family people mover that was full of rubbish and smelt slightly of dog. She realised to her surprise that the golden retriever, Bobby, was not the only one coming with them, but also Frau König's daughter, Lena. She would have thought the girl would be hanging around in the mall at the Red Main Centre rather than going on an excursion to a plant exchange.

When Doris let fall a remark to this effect, Lena giggled and said, "Don't worry, I'm not going to be looking for flowers with you. I'm meeting up with Lisa and Anna because we have to do a group project for school."

This restored the equilibrium of Doris Lech's view of the world.

"Lisa? Her last name's not Kerner, by any chance?"

"Yes it is – do you know her? Of course, Lisa's sister works for the police as well," said Lena, answering her own question.

Lisa's sister was no one else but Lotte, Doris' bubbly assistant. Doris had seen Lisa, who looked the spitting image of Lotte, at the garlic festival.

Frau König smiled and said, "Bayreuth sure is a village, everyone knows everyone else."

Yes, Doris was already well aware of this. It seemed as if an invisible web had been spun right across the town, entwining every inhabitant, with strands stretching out into the surrounding countryside. Once again, Doris felt herself an outsider, a stranger here too. Lotte Kerner at least was going all out to change that. From day one, she had made no secret of the fact that she wanted to integrate her boss into the Bayreuth community as quickly as possible. Doris herself could well remember their first meeting, when she had rather stiffly and clumsily tried to find the right words for the occasion. Even though Doris was senior to Lotte at work and the older of the two, Lotte had not bothered to wait for her to speak first but had right away gone against convention and offered to shake hands. She then promptly introduced herself, another who habitually spoke in the strong local dialect.

"Well, I'm Lotte" – which actually sounded like 'Lodde' in dialect – "and I'm happy to fill you in on everything there is to know about Bayreuth, so you can settle in as quickly as possible and become one of us. Have you got anything on this evening? No? Well, you can come along with me, and I'll show you Bayreuth by night."

Now, Bayreuth by night, outside the Wagner Festival and the semester holidays, was truly unspectacular. That night, however, had been something special. In particular, it had marked the beginning of an unusual friendship. And friends were something Doris truly and urgently needed after her ostracism in Cologne.

Doris was torn from her thoughts when her landlady brought the conversation round to the upcoming school anniversary. The Richard Wagner Grammar School, known as RWG for short, and also dubbed, admittedly by those inhabitants of Bayreuth who were already showing plenty of grey hair, as the 'broomstick stable', had already notched up a respectable 150 years, a milestone that was leading to plenty of celebrations. One of the high points of the anniversary was a theatre production that was going to include Lena. Her mother reported this with suitable enthusiasm, while Lena anxiously averted her gaze.

"Mum! You don't really think Frau Lech is going to be interested? It's not that exciting, you know," Lena protested reproachfully from the back seat. Doris hurried to contradict her.

"No, Lena – of course I'm interested. Would you like to tell me what the play is about?"

"Well, what plays are always about – love and betrayal."

Frau König couldn't manage to keep her mouth shut.

"Imagine, Frau Lech, the play is already 100 years old. A teacher cleaning up around the school found an old trunk with costumes and the script of the play – handwritten – inside! Just imagine! I can't read the old-fashioned handwriting, it's like spiders' legs, just scribble. What did you say it's called, Lena?"

Once more an exasperated sigh came from the back.

"The play or the handwriting? The handwriting is called German cursive and teachers have to be able to read it. Frau Grimm typed all of it out for us; it was a lot of work. And the play is called 'Dance of the Elves' – complete kitsch. It's set a hundred years ago. This guy goes to the war, he's called Georg Ludwig. And he's in love with an Anna Maria. Another guy is in love with her as well, a Konrad von Something. And because Konrad's a noble and has influence, he makes sure that Georg Ludwig is sent on a suicide mission and is killed. Anna Maria then gets engaged to Konrad, but she finds out he has Georg on his conscience. And then she kills first Konrad and then herself."

Doris made an extra effort to sound interested.

"And the play has already been performed once before, more than a hundred years ago? That must have been for the fiftieth anniversary of the school? What a lovely idea!"

Lena snorted audibly. "If only! You haven't got it quite right, Frau Lech. In the trunk there was also an old newspaper with a death notice, of a certain Margarethe Schlehmüller. She in fact lived near here."

Frau König butted in again.

"We're actually going to drive past Blackthorn Mill where Margarethe Schlehmüller lived. I'll point it out when we do."

"Anyway, Margarethe died at our school. She was supposed to have thrown herself from the clock tower, and because she was somehow involved in the play, the whole production was then cancelled. There was a note from her teacher in the trunk. It said the girl apparently killed herself because she had lost her father and two of her brothers in the war and a third brother had gone missing. She had not had the strength to bear it. The whole business was certainly desperately sad. In any case, one evening she was found lying at the bottom of the tower. Frau Grimm said that, in those days, suicides were not buried in the cemetery, but somewhere else, and not even buried by a pastor. The poor mother."

Now Doris showed genuine interest. The story sounded like a small scandal. She wondered if and how the police had investigated suicides at the time? There were hardly any forensic methods then to distinguish suicide from murder. And in the confusion of the war, it was rather questionable, in any case, how far the police could have followed the rules of investigation. Who knows what sort of cases would have come up on a daily basis? And certainly, manpower would have been tight, even tighter than today.

"Have you ever tried to find out more exact details about this Margarethe? Or her family?"

Lena shrugged her shoulders.

"There are no Schlehmüllers still living in Blackthorn Mill. But our class did a study of school history and found out that the girl was in the same year level as some people who are still known today. Zweistein for example. Does the name mean anything to you?"

"Well, it's a rather common name," Doris replied jokingly.

But Lena, unresponsive to irony, replied, "Not in Bayreuth, where the name Zweistein stands straight behind Wagner and Liszt. Albert Zweistein is supposed to have written a sonata that at the time was an enormous success. He was just a one-hit-wonder, though, since he didn't live much longer, dying in his twenties from – what did they call it in those days – that's right, consumption. Frau Grimm says that all diseases that couldn't be identified were called consumption back then. Anyway, this Albert's sister, a Lisette Zweistein, was in the same year as Margarethe. It is quite possible that they even went to and from school together. The Zweisteins lived in Wolfsbach …"

Again, her mother butted in.

"They still live there; they have an enormous block that used to be their country estate. They've got money to burn. Half of Wolfsbach belongs to them. Frau Lech, you're going to come to the show, aren't you? Lena can reserve you a ticket. You'll get to know half of Bayreuth in one fell swoop. Even the Wagners are meant to be coming."

"Mama! The Wagners aren't the centre of the universe, however much you go on about them."

Doris jumped at mention of the Wagners.

"Well, yes, perhaps they aren't the centre of the universe, but I'd still find it interesting to meet them. And your play sounds well worth seeing. It would be really nice of you if you could get me a ticket, Lena. When is it exactly?"

Lena creased her forehead as she tried to remember. "Mind like a sieve – the performances are sometime in mid-October. Wait a minute, I've got the date on my phone … yes, here: the performances are on the 11th, 12th, and 13th October. Wednesday to Friday. When would it suit you best?"

"Hmmm, the premiere is on Wednesday, and I imagine it will be full to bursting. Preferably on Thursday, okay?"

"Then you certainly won't get to see the Wagners. They are only guaranteed to come to the premiere."

Doris smiled. "It doesn't matter. The next Wagner Festival will come around soon enough and I'm determined to get tickets."

In the meantime, they had arrived in Emtmannsberg and Frau König had parked the people mover on the curb of a narrow street behind a row of other vehicles. The plant exchange was apparently a favourite place to meet. Bobby got out hesitantly and sniffed the lamppost. Lena clipped on his lead. "I'm taking him along to Lisa. And I can go home with Anna's parents. Ciao!"

Doris hoped for Anna's parents' sake that they also owned a dog – she wouldn't want either the dog's hair or the slight but stubborn doggy smell in her own car. Frau König had already surged ahead, so Doris hurried to follow her into a small courtyard. At the gate there was a piggybank for donations – the plants themselves were free. A wide selection of plants was spread out over a closely mown lawn and surrounds. Everything from gladioli to asters to evening primroses was represented, along with several plants that Doris had not seen before. As she bent over a green tuft, a man in a garden apron stepped next to her.

"That is a mountain knapweed. It blooms in May with a dark blue flower, a real beauty."

Doris looked up in surprise.

"Walter Kremnitz. If you have any questions, just ask."

"Oh, you know, I'm actually only looking for indoor plants. I'm Doris Lech. I'm here with Frau König."

She pointed in the direction of her landlady.

"Frau König – yes, she comes here every year. If you want to have coffee and cake later, then take a look at our photo wall; you'll find her in plenty of the photos. But for now, you're after indoor plants – they're all on the steps of the tool shed, over there. Today we've got several different cacti, one big and two small weeping figs, two anthuriums, clivias – they have a beautiful orange flower – even a big monstera and an asparagus fern. And scented geraniums – they keep the flies away."

Doris raised her eyebrows. She felt herself a bit over-whelmed by the variety.

"An asparagus fern? What sort of asparagus is that?" she wanted to know.

Kremnitz ran to the garden shed.

"Here, this is it. An asparagus fern. It's not for eating, it's an ornamental asparagus. It goes well in the bathroom, perhaps in combination with one or two other ferns?"

Doris thanked him and quietly inspected the range on offer, while her landlady, a broad, enthusiastic smile on her face, loaded up the car with the plants she had chosen. Doris found it hard to decide. She wanted something big and green in the living room, but she shied away from taking up half of the car, reluctantly turning away with a sigh from the big green monstera and its variegated small friends.

Frau König stepped up to her unnoticed, having observed Doris' hesitation.

"Frau Lech, if you want the big monstera, it's no problem. We can fit it in if we lay down the back seats. After all, there's only the two of us on the trip back."

Doris still needed some coaxing, but then Walter Kremnitz appeared again and after heartily greeting her landlady set about trying to convince Doris.

"What isn't snapped up today will freeze tomorrow night; frost is forecast, and we don't have anywhere to keep the indoor plants under cover. Load the monstera in the car, and both those small colourful ones had better go with them."

With that it became clear that Doris could not bring herself to leave the pots behind at the mercy of the frost. Kremnitz dragged the big plant to the car, while Doris carried the two small ones.

As Frau König closed the tailgate, Kremnitz nodded contentedly.

"And now you ladies have to come along and meet my wife. Angelika is inside selling cakes. There's plum cake, made from our own plums, cheesecake, Black Forest cherry cake, apple cake, and if you're lucky, there will still be a bit of banana Swiss roll left."

Frau König elbowed Doris in the ribs.

"Banana Swiss roll! Be quick, it's fabulous."

4

1917

The girls ran laughing and joking out of the gymnasium into the theatre storeroom. They were all the same age, what was then called 'baked fish age' in Germany. At that same age, their grandchildren's generation would be known as 'teenagers', but understandably the 'baked fish' did not know that at the time. They giggled, elbowing each other in the ribs as they pulled on their costumes, old-fashioned clothes with ankle-length dark blue woollen skirts and white cotton tops trimmed with broad sailor collars. Added to that were dark knitted hats that in another setting would not have looked out of place on a French bon vivant. All of them were excited because today the parts for the most important stage play since the founding of the school were going to be given out. It was to be performed for the school anniversary of what was then known as the 'Higher Daughters' School' – on the quiet, disrespectfully called the 'broomstick stable' by the citizens of Bayreuth – and everyone of rank and title in Bayreuth was expected to attend. It was announced that, alongside the mayor, von Casselmann, and a few other illustrious members of the masonic lodge, none other than Siegfried Wagner, the son of Richard Wagner, the celebrated composer who would later give his name to the school, would attend with his wife, Winifred.

Of course, it wouldn't be a light-hearted festival; the times were far too grim for that. There was hardly a family that was not mourning someone who had died in the war, hardly anyone for whom things were really going well. The news a few months ago that America had joined the Allied Powers in declaring war on Germany did not smooth the wrinkles on anyone's brow. The continuous battles had already lasted too long for anyone to believe in a victory. Citizens quietly whispered about the senselessness of the war, about how much they longed for an end to the catastrophe. The girls, 14, 15 or 16 years old, could hardly imagine things being any different than how they were now – youth forgets quickly – but neither were they happy.

The stage play promised a change and a distraction from gloomy thoughts and allowed the young things to ignore their rumbling stomachs. And so, they giggled and fooled around so excessively that eventually their teacher, Fräulein Schmittig, clapped her ruler on the wooden desk and loudly called for the girls to discipline themselves.

"Ladies, I very much hope that you are clear about one thing: only girls who demonstrate, on the day, firstly, flawless performances and, secondly, flawless manners, will be allowed to participate. Running around honking like geese doesn't make the grade. So please, moderate your silly behaviour before I'm forced to do something about it."

Covert whispering persisted for a moment before quiet returned. Fräulein Schmittig smiled with satisfaction and then went on, "I would firstly like to give some basic information about our play. It's called 'Dance of the Elves' and it revolves around love, betrayal, war and death –"

A hand shot up.

"Yes, Lisette? What is it?"

Lisette grinned broadly and asked in an innocent voice, "If the play is about love and war – will students from the Boys' High School perform too? It sounds as if male parts will be needed."

A renewed burst of giggling echoed through the gymnasium. Some girls went red, others gently nudged each other. Fräulein Schmittig tried to remain serious.

"Lisette, I have to disappoint you. Like always, this year all the male parts will be played by you girls. If you want to meet students from the Boys' High School, then go walking in the palace garden on Sundays. Perhaps you'll have more luck there than here."

Now Lisette turned red as well and stuffed the end of her plait in her mouth to chew on it in embarrassment.

"Good. Back to our play. We have fourteen parts to cast. All those who want a part need to audition now. So that things run smoothly, I would like to mention that good marks will be taken into consideration when there are more applicants than parts to be played. But you already know all this from previous years. Here are the parts; make yourselves familiar with them – at three o'clock, that is, in half an hour, the auditions will begin."

The girls stuck their heads into the scripts and immersed themselves in the roles.

Fräulein Schmittig used the quiet moment to go up to a student who was standing somewhat to one side.

"Margarethe, I've something rather special planned for you. I would love it if you took over the musical accompaniment to 'Dance of the Elves'. You play the piano so beautifully that it would really enhance the play. Would you like to?"

Margarethe Schlehmüller did not have to think about it for long. She knew that neither her marks nor her acting ability were really outstanding. No more than a small bit part would be in it for her. On top of that, her father had been killed in action in March. The year of mourning was still not past. Who knew if her mother would even let her perform? It really would not be proper. But when she played the piano, then she was in her own world, a world where she moved with the certainty of a sleepwalker. Just the notion that she would be able to play music again was enticing enough. She enthusiastically agreed.

"I'd like to very, very much, Fräulein Schmittig. I'd really love that. There's just one problem. We don't have a piano anymore. My mother sold it to buy winter firewood and two hens. Eggs have become more important than music."

The teacher looked at her, taken aback. Everywhere the same story. Piece by piece what was left of a better past existence was being sold or exchanged to ensure survival. She sighed. It wasn't worth thinking about; how many talents had withered unrecognised and unused, unnamed casualties of the war, let alone all the talent that had died on the battlefields. Such senseless killing and dying that had plunged a whole country, no, a whole world into misery. But, of course, it could never be said aloud.

"Margarethe, I'm sure you'll be able to practise on our school grand piano in the Blue Grotto. I'll talk to Herr Schulz first thing in the morning. He will certainly have no objections. And then you can practise for as long as you want after school."

Margarethe smiled in gratitude. To be allowed to play music again! A dream come true. She had cried so many hot tears longing for this moment. She was sure that her father would now be looking down on her from heaven and rejoicing with her. He had loved music as much as she did and had given her lessons when he had time left over from privately tutoring various daughters of the landed gentry. Her mother had never understood, had never shared this passion. Otherwise, she would have known that both Margarethe and her father, Rudolf, would rather have frozen and gone hungry than sell the piano. Oh daddy, if you were only still here …

Her teacher's voice tore her away from her daydreams.

"I was thinking of a long piece for the overture, then, in several places in the production, light background music. And to finish, when the curtain falls, again a longer piece. Wagner, naturally, that goes without saying, but not only Richard – I will get in touch with Siegfried Wagner and ask if he has composed a piano piece that might be suitable. And I would also like some Liszt, for the love scene, when Georg Ludwig confesses his feelings to Anna Maria before he goes off to the war. He turns away from her after pleading with her to wait for him – what could be more suitable than 'Liebestraum'? Best you start practising 'Liebestraum' tomorrow. I'll bring along the other pieces in the course of the week."

Margarethe nodded obediently without mentioning that she could play 'Liebestraum' by heart. She was excited about the other pieces. And she knew what she would practise as well …

While the other girls muttered their parts sotto voce to themselves, Margarethe sat crossed legged in a corner on the floor. Her mother would certainly not have been pleased. Neither being on the floor, nor the way of sitting was proper for a young girl. But sitting there like that was the best way to think, to concentrate. Margarethe closed her eyes and imagined the melody of 'Liebestraum'. It wasn't particularly difficult for her to let the written music appear to her inner eye. Margarethe's fingers began to twitch, silently playing the imagined notes. The murmuring of her schoolmates became softer and trailed almost completely away. Instead, Margarethe now heard quite clearly what she was playing. She still knew how to play 'Liebestraum', still knew where the difficult bits were hidden. And even in her silent playing, she played the same wrong chord she used to play on the piano, which, naturally enough, she also heard and noticed.

Lisette nudged her friend Käthe and pointed to Margarethe. The two watched their classmate for a few seconds before they giggled and went back to their text.

Margarethe did not notice. She was immersed in a completely different world.

5

Tina Hermann looked somewhat nervous as she glanced at her expensive gold watch. Ten past one – as per usual her boss was stretching lunch out considerably longer than needed. Attorney Dr Held had disappeared into town as early as half past eleven. Going out the door he had called back his usual excuse, '*lunch* with Judge Salesch', referring to the now well out of date courtroom show on German television, and then smirked like a schoolboy at the bad joke. Tina had forced a smile for the sake of politeness but knew exactly how fake it looked.

Dr Held had also yelled over his shoulder: "Please don't ring me while I'm at lunch. I can be reached again in an hour."

Tina had briefly toyed with the idea of following her boss. Perhaps it would have been worth it, perhaps she would have found out something that she could blackmail him with. But she dismissed the idea – Dr Held certainly earned enough, but in contrast to the people whose racy details she had saved to her laptop, he was small fry who really was not worth extorting.

Anyway, today Tina was holding fort in chambers completely by herself because the secretary, Frau Mauser, had reported sick. Tina could leaf through all manner of files undisturbed, and she purposefully looked for what appeared interesting. 'Crystal Spa' stood out on many thick files full of correspondence. Dr Held had little time for the much-lauded paperless office: 'All this nonsense with electronic data processing – you have to be able to physically lay your hands on information', was his motto. As a result, he had refused for years to let more technology than was absolutely necessary into chambers. And as for Frau Mauser, a prematurely aged, dried out, former beauty, now about to retire, her computer phobia made her fit in perfectly. Tina had shaken her head with its luxurious blond mane often enough at so much ignorance. Nevertheless, in this case, such ignorance was helpful. If Dr Held had password protected all his active files, she would not have found it so easy to access all the insider knowledge she was so greedily looking for. It was not the first time she had pulled out her phone to take snapshots of files. But today she could relax and pursue her illegal activities without risking being caught out by Frau Mauser, whose already rather short midday breaks were becoming even shorter to make a good impression on her boss. Laughable. Mauser would have at the most two years ahead of her before retirement – as if Dr Held would let her go then, anyway. Poor old thing, Tina thought to herself, obviously she had no other interests.

Never, never, never did she want to end up like her. She wanted to live, really live the high life. She would have easily been able to imagine a life like that at Albert's side. And Phil? Irritated, she pushed this thought aside. Albert and Phil were not worth wasting unnecessary time on. No, they were only worth a thorough and precise investigation, however much Tina's feelings might get in the way. The intern lawyer energetically leafed through the pages of files she had taken out of the filing cabinets, took snapshots again and again with her phone, put files back and took out other files. Yes, today had been a successful day, and the laxative she had put in Mauser's end of day coffee yesterday had been a good investment.

But now she had been sitting around doing nothing for just on half an hour, because she had to reckon with Dr Held's return. She drummed on the tabletop with her perfectly manicured fingernails and, as idly waiting around became too much for her, after a brief hesitation she rang a friend.

"Hi, Sara, have you got time to chat. I'm sitting here in the office – the boss isn't here, Mauser is sick, nothing to do … Yeah, exactly, I'm bored to death. Just have a look out of the window – in beautiful weather like this you should be playing golf, not sitting around inside … Oh, don't be so petty bourgeois. And whether or not it would be fun, you have to try it at least once. Why am I ringing? Would you like to go on a short trip to Rome? On the weekend? … No, Phil isn't coming. Right now, he is in his studio in Milan. I'm hardly ever seeing him at the moment … Yes, lots to do for the spring collection … What? It's a bit late for next year? Sara, dear, for the year after next, not next year … Yes, of course I'm up with the new fashions. Come with me to Rome, then there'll be enough time for me to tell you everything while we're shopping … Money, money … what do you mean you've got no money? Do you think I've got enough just lying around? I've made sure I've got a credit card, you can too. And then we can make a side trip to Monaco, to the casino, perhaps we'll have luck and win … Oh, come on! … No, I haven't changed, I'm still the same old Tina. I only want to experience things, see something of the world. Think about it, I would really love to. Oh-oh – must fly, my boss is arriving."

Tina's call to her friend Sara had only taken a few minutes but always, when you least wanted him to, Dr Held turned up on the doormat. Once again, Tina felt deeply annoyed by her internship. Studying law, that wasn't who she was – she had already realised that after only a few semesters. Only, what else should she do? Tina wished she would win the lottery, to finally be able to afford the life she dreamed about. Oh, to be able to buy Phil off, that good-looking arsehole with the good manners and the slippery character. To begin anew with

Albert, once again right from the start, this time honestly and sincerely. If it were only that easy. Tina knew well enough that such hopes were fanciful. Albert had used her and betrayed her once; he would do it again. It was not worth wasting even a single thought on him. And Phil, he wasn't for nothing Albert's best friend. He had been a gambler in this nasty wager, and she had been the stake. How stupid of her to think it had all been about feelings. No matter, what's done is done, she thought. Only that, in the meantime, she had learnt to gamble herself, and she intended to play for high stakes. She had very good cards and she would win, thanks to Dr Held.

Reluctantly, Tina picked up the files she had already put into the right order and went out to take them to her boss. Nothing was worse than going into a meeting unprepared; Mauser had preached that to her on her very first day. Tina paused a moment at the half open door of her boss's office. He was already back on the phone, presumably with his date from midday, something that brought a smirk to her face. She was just on the point of bursting in when she became aware of his business-like tone of voice. Mauser's Sermon Number 2 – never disturb the boss during a business call. There was no official, hard and fast rule about overhearing these types of calls, so Tina used the grey area generously to her own benefit. Dr Held sounded slightly ill at ease as he obviously prepared himself for a long monologue.

"You know, we've already gone over this more than once. No, of course I believed you from the start. Yes, I know you heard the whole story from your great aunt when you were still a little girl. And, of course, it's a very good thing that the old lady wrote it all down properly, and, of course, I believe you that she heard it all from Frau Hagen, who in turn claimed to have heard it first-hand. But that's not enough evidence for us, not cut and dried proof that the score Zweistein published had been written by someone else. What we are missing is the dubious dedication you say proves your allegation. Without that we simply can't do anything. And even then, it is questionable whether your great aunt's letter can be seen as legally admissible evidence. It doesn't matter if it says the Zweisteins committed fraud twenty times. First of all, all the members of the Wagner family would probably have their say before you. I would suggest a better course of action is to go step by step. Locate the dedication and then we can consider taking it further. There's no point spending vast amounts of money to have the letter legally certified when, even then, it won't be of any help … Yes, Frau Weigelt, I know the whole story, and I can well understand that you feel utterly betrayed. But it's now already a long time ago and if we want to get anywhere, we need the dedication. At the very least. And even then … Yes, I hope you have a nice day, too."

Tina quickly drew back two steps, preventing Held from catching her eavesdropping. But she could not suppress a contented grin. She recognised the name Zweistein, and she could put two and two together from what her boss had said. Might it be new ammunition that she could use to her benefit at the right moment?

She strode up to the door, gave a quick, strong knock, pushed herself through the opening and lay the files on the desk.

"Hello Dr Held, here is the Mayer case for 2:00 pm. Can I do anything else for you?"

Dr Held glanced up and smiled briefly without really noticing she was there.

"No thanks. But if you could please arrange for fresh coffee when the Mayers come. After that you can go home for the day. There's nothing more scheduled and Frau Mauser is not here to explain anything to you."

Tina gave a pleased nod and murmured, "Thank you, Dr Held, that is nice of you," before she went to go out again.

She was almost in the corridor when Dr Held, obviously having remembered something, called after her.

"Isn't it unbelievable how people sometimes clutch at straws when pecuniary interests are involved?"

"What do you mean?" Tina wanted to know, irritated by her boss saying 'pecuniary interests' when he meant 'money'.

He played with his pen, seemingly lost in thought, clicking it incessantly up and down. When he spoke again it sounded as if he was talking to himself.

"Greed changes people, brings out sides of them that you would never have guessed. I've known Frau Weigelt for decades, but since she found the letter from her late aunt, she has become totally obsessed by the desire to ruin the Zweistein family. Old Albert Zweistein wrote a famous piano sonata about a hundred years ago that brought in a tidy sum in royalties as film music for a supernova."

Tina would have liked to know what he meant by a 'supernova'. Wasn't a supernova an exploding star? But she held back, not wanting to interrupt. What he was saying was too tantalising.

"And the Zweisteins spent the money, among other things, on a good deal of land around their estate in Wolfsbach, which is now a housing development. Frau Weigelt, for her part distantly related to the Wagner clan from Green Hill, has the fixed idea that Albert didn't write the sonata himself but, on the contrary, Siegfried Wagner was the composer. If that were true, then it would be conceivable to bring an action against the Zweisteins. It works out like this: a large part of the land that the Zweisteins bought was previously in possession of Frau Weigelt's parents; the Zweisteins had at that time systematically brought about the ruin of the Weigelts and had bought the land for next to nothing; and now it's to become a new housing development – perhaps you've heard of Storchennest II?

"Well, it's understandable that someone would feel cheated and even want to have a piece of the cake. Particularly since the Zweisteins have really ostentatiously displayed the wealth they got from the sonata. I was there once. They have a whole salon for Albert's piano. It can even still be played. And right above it the original sheet music hangs on the wall, expensively framed. Naturally, not the original, at least I presume not. That would be sacrilege; it would fade in no time. Anyway, when the planned rezoning was first published in the *Courier*, Frau Weigelt started ringing me day and night. Unfortunately, the good lady did not have any proof for her allegations. It's hard to believe – before all this she was a happy enough woman. And now she is eaten up by hate and greed. Draw your own lessens from that, Fräulein Hermann."

Fräulein! Who still says Fräulein these days?

"And always keep in the forefront of your mind that people are sometimes happier without great wealth."

Tina reflected for a moment.

"This proposed housing development at Wolfsbach, isn't that the land that is actually proposed as a nature reserve, because of the wild orchids and some other rare plants that have been found there?"

"You're well informed. I hadn't expected that of you at all, that you would be so concerned with nature conservation. You're right, wild orchids have been found there, they're highly protected. The Federation of Nature Conservation has fought hard for this land to be identified as a nature reserve. And for a while, things looked to be going well, right up until the city's building committee decided otherwise and suddenly wanted to re-examine the Zweistein's application for rezoning. The Zweistein's would have benefited either way – there would have been compensation payments from the Federation – but now it is more likely to be valued at construction land prices. Are you active in nature conservation?"

He looked his intern student in the face with interest. It appeared as if he had a soft spot for environmental activists. But Tina had to disappoint him.

"No, no. God forbid! That isn't my thing. But I've got a girlfriend who is studying biology, and she is very active and interested in everything that happens around here regarding the environment. She's told me all about it in the minutest detail. In fact, she herself has participated in surveys of amphibian numbers and has recorded toad populations."

That was only half the story but the whole story was none of her boss's business.

Disappointment deeply etched Dr Held's face.

"Well, you should take a page out of your friend's book and be more active in working to protect our world. One day you will have children of your own and you'll want to leave them a world worth living in."

Without waiting for an answer, the attorney reached for the file folder that was lying on the desk in front of him and Tina went back across to her little cubbyhole. She mechanically put on the coffee and stared at the groaning coffee machine without really noticing it rattling. No, her boss was wrong! Life was definitely better with money than without. She could well understand Frau Weigelt. And, incidentally, perhaps this information would also be helpful to her – admittedly not straight away, but who knew? Perhaps in time …

6

Bayreuth, Spring 2017

Tina Hermann sighed. She had absolutely no desire to go out with her friend, Sara, but a promise was a promise. Sara wanted to belatedly celebrate her birthday, which was difficult to refuse. Rosenau! As if that would do! Comfortably lounging at home on the sofa and reading an exciting book, that would be great, just in leggings and a sweatshirt, with a cup of tea, a few candles, a packet of chips. That would be Tina's idea of a pleasant evening – not stuck in a crowd listening to loud music. But she could not get out of this one. So, she exchanged her favourite grey hoodie for a tank top and light open blouse on top of tight jeans. She only put on the bare minimum of makeup but let her ponytail fall away to wear her long blond hair loose. When she showed up at Sara's for aperitifs, several girls from her year level had arrived before her and all were already tipsy. That was another thing that she could not understand or bear. Why did you have to pump yourself full of alcohol to the point of passing out to have fun? Tina frowned but put a good face on it and drank a glass of prosecco. That was it though – she did not plan on losing control. Rather, she was intrigued by the deterioration in her girlfriends. Unbelievable what alcohol did to people. Tina was both fascinated and repelled.

She would have preferred to turn on her heel and flee back home to the sofa, but Sara announced airily, "Off we go to

Rosi!" and the giggling gaggle got on their feet to make their way to their favourite haunt in Badstraße.

Out of place. That was precisely the expression for how Tina felt. She desperately held onto her glass of cola so that no one could slip something into it unobserved. Oh my God, it was so boring! She could never understand this desire to go out. Even today, on Sara's birthday, she waited desperately for the moment when she could make an inconspicuous getaway. Suddenly, she felt a hand on her shoulder and someone, so as to be understood over the loud music, yelled in her ear.

"I've never seen you here before. I'm Albert. Let's dance?"

Indignant, Tina shook the hand off and looked angrily at the guy. She hated being chatted up like that. But when she looked into his eyes, something strange happened to her. All of a sudden, she no longer heard the roaring music. People swirled around her in slow motion and her annoyance was blown away.

Without really wanting to, she answered, "I'd rather we went outside, it's too loud in here."

And amazingly this fairy-tale prince, who must have come from another dimension, nodded and went ahead of her out to the carpark. Tina could not do anything but stare at him in fascination. She did not know how it had happened to her; she only knew that she had been struck by lightning. This Albert wouldn't have to say another word – she would follow him anywhere, unconditionally. He was of average height, tanned, with dark blond locks and blue eyes. His white teeth sparkled in straight rows. His voice sounded like soft velvet and when he laughed, she felt a tingle inside. It told in his favour that he did not immediately exploit her state of totally obvious stupid infatuation, but just talked to her. She spoke truthfully of Sara's birthday and how annoyed she was by the evening and how she actually just wanted to leave.

Albert laughed softly, and Tina trembled in the pit of her stomach.

"Go? Already? okay – my place or yours?"

Saying this he traced his index finger as light as a feather over her chin, from her dimple downwards, along her neck and over her collarbone. Tina felt herself fainting, but Albert picked her up and she suddenly found herself in a passionate embrace with an utterly strange man. Again, she felt herself falling into an abyss but was raised up again by his kisses, swirling up in ecstatic pirouettes to unimagined heights, all thought turned off.

Finally, between two kisses, his words trickled into her consciousness.

"Hey, you haven't answered me, your place or mine?"

Tina pushed the man a little away from her.

"I don't go home with just any guy – if I only know his first name and nothing else," she said, trying to put up a last, weak resistance. But again, he just laughed and that was enough.

"If that's all it is – Zweistein, Albert Zweistein. Resident in Wolfsbach, profession, doctor. Single child, unmarried, no hereditary diseases. Do you want to know anything else?"

Tina heard the metallic click of a car lock and then found herself sitting in the passenger seat of a red Porsche travelling into the night that would change her life forever.

7

It was already late afternoon when the young girls left the school. They chattered excitedly among themselves. Margarethe, who had not taken part in the auditions, thought about how she had been chosen to do the musical accompaniment. As Fräulein Schmittig had earlier let it be known, the parts had been given out, in the first instance, not on the basis of talent, but rather on the basis of grades – and, Margarethe guessed, on the basis of family influence. Even if no one would have said it openly, when in doubt, the daughter of a rich family got the role. And Margarethe secretly asked herself if such decisions required a generous donation. But that, thank God, had not applied to her. Fräulein Schmittig was so convinced of her musical talent that, in her case, no competition emerged.

The role of Anna Maria as the main female part had naturally been hotly contested, as had been its male counterpart. Seven girls alone had competed for the role of Anna Maria. That Lisette had won the race had not really surprised Margarethe. Lisette was one of the few girls who was still given a packed lunch when she left the house in the early morning. Her wealthy, influential father owned a large estate at Wolfsbach, which meant that she always had enough to eat. As well, Lisette was driven into town every day in a carriage.

That was the main reason Margarethe made sure she stayed in her good books, as getting a lift in the carriage to Wolfsbach saved her a long walk home. Even so, she still had to trudge a fair way from where she was dropped off to get to where she lived in Blackthorn Mill.

Despite going to school together, the pair were not close friends. What Margarethe did not know, however, was that Lisette's father, the old round-bellied lord of the manor, made sure Margarethe's opportunity to get a lift was paid for in his way, once a week seeking out Blackthorn Mill when Margarethe and her brother were out of the house ...

Before Margarethe's father had been conscripted, Lisette had also been one of his students, as had her elder brother, Albert. Margarethe's father never spoke of his students, but from the curt observations he let slip from time to time, Margarethe knew precisely what musical talent the siblings had: moderate in Albert's case, hopelessly unmusical in Lisette's.

In the end, this had led to conflict between the two fathers because Albert's father naturally blamed the piano teacher for Lisette's ham-fisted piano playing. Rudolf had started teaching Lisette more than five years before, and before that, for several years, he had had Albert as a student. Albert had struck him as at least an adequate student.

As Albert matured, his father decided one day, on the spur of the moment, that piano playing was not for real men, and, as a result, Albert had found himself on the shooting range at the rifle club instead of in front of the piano in the drawing room of the manor house. Already at that time, there had been cause for conflict between the two men, since Rudolf, who felt sorry for the visibly unhappy Albert, had tried in vain to stand up for him.

Margarethe naturally knew nothing of the hidden reasons that had led Albert's father to make his decision. Her father, on the other hand, had known with certainty that Albert's father had been driven by fear and worry. It had not eluded

Rudolf that Albert evinced a rather feminine manner and had drawn his own absolutely correct conclusions, without knowing that there was a specific reason for the ban on piano playing. One day, when Albert was home alone, his father had unexpectedly returned home early and caught his son in front of his mother's wardrobe wearing makeup and squeezed into a corset. He had made sure nothing became public but had taken matters into his own hands to turn his boy into a 'real man'. Next to learning to know his way around weapons, a visit to an out of the way house was included, where men on entering threw a few coins into a jar before they slipped into an adjoining room …

Rudolf, who, after that, only taught Lisette, only met Albert when coming and going, and worried about the young man. Albert had become cynical. He had emerged from his father's re-education measures like a phoenix out of the ashes, and had, because of them, left behind all the friendliness and warmheartedness that had once been the nicest things about him.

Rudolf presumed that Albert would shortly be forced to marry, so his father could persuade himself that his measures had been successful. Rudolf strongly doubted it. But what did it have to do with him? He was only the piano teacher, who was failing because of Lisette's lack of talent. Twice a week he had to make an appearance at the manor and have his ears assaulted for an hour before being allowed to disappear again. At least he had been paid well for it, since Albert's father was no tightwad when he was convinced of the point of something he was paying for. But, eventually, he too had to admit that Lisette's playing sounded ghastly, and that no afternoon tea visitor could be expected to find it uplifting entertainment. As a proud father, far from agreeing with Rudolf, he was convinced that this situation had come about not because of his daughter's lack of talent but because of the lack of talent of the piano teacher. And because of that, Rudolf had lost his well-paid position at Wolfsbach. As it turned out, losing his position had not mattered, because, just a few days later, he had been conscripted into the armed forces and sent to the front, where, after only a short while, he had been killed.

More fateful was the fact that Albert's father – irritated by the feeling that he was being extorted for a reason he kept secret, but also coveting another man's wife – had paid a visit to a good acquaintance in the War Office and had pushed an envelope across the desk that contained a certain sum of money and a slip of paper on which the name of a man was written, a man who, up until then, had had his enlistment deferred, a name that the alert reader will certainly have already guessed …

8

It was about two weeks later that a damper was put on Tina's intoxicating infatuation. She had not spent one evening, not one night without Albert since Sara's birthday. He had waited on her hand and foot. He had sent her romantic messages several times a day. On Sunday, a florist delivery of an enormous bouquet of red roses arrived unexpectedly on her doorstep – Tina's mother had stared stunned at the delivery man and it had taken several seconds before she had realised that the flowers were for her daughter and not for her. Naturally, Tina was mercilessly pumped for information, but she did not allow herself to reveal more than that there was a new man in her life, who she would soon certainly introduce to her mother and father in person.

Tina was on cloud nine, already secretly dreaming of a shared future with Albert. She had been taken to swanky restaurants, had gone with him to a concert in Nuremberg, and he had bought her a gorgeous, beautiful summer dress. She would have loved most of all to have a corner of his bathroom cupboard reserved for her and had already stored a few important items there permanently, but Albert had not said anything about them, and she had not dared ask.

Finally, on a Tuesday evening, she turned up to see him in Wolfsbach as soon as he had finished work, but today he made no move to leave the house again.

"Come on, Tina, let's stay in today. I'm too tired to do anything too strenuous. Let's just get pizza delivered. That'll be great. Besides, I'm planning something special with you today ..."

Once again, he looked at her so intensely that she trembled in the pit of her stomach and would have done anything for him on the spot. Then his gaze wandered in the direction of the bedroom, and she racked her brain to guess what he could have planned that would top the last few nights.

She then remembered she had promised her mother she would introduce this dream man to her and her father as soon as possible.

"Okay, agreed. But you must promise me something in return, that you don't plan anything for this Friday evening except to come to my place for dinner. My parents are dying to meet you."

A gentle smile spread across Albert's face, his features reflecting eager anticipation.

"If we're still together on Friday, then fine," he laughed.

Tina flinched. What did he mean by that? Was he planning on dropping her? When Albert saw the shock on her face, he kissed her tenderly on the tip of her nose.

"No panic. I'm not going to put an end to it. But do you already know that you won't?"

"Nonsense – why would I? I'm much too much in love with you," Tina blurted out and blushed slightly. She had never said it openly, but it was glaringly obvious. Albert pulled her firmly to him and began to kiss her passionately, but that was his only response, and a tiny doubt began almost imperceptibly to gnaw at her.

An hour later the pizza was delivered. It was only luke-warm but despite that, the best pizza Tina had ever eaten – obviously love not only makes you blind, it also kills off your tastebuds. Now she was really curious about what Albert was planning for her for the evening. When she spoke about it, he laughed again and, as always in such moments, she felt as if she would swoon, and he would catch her and carry her off to bed. Never in her life had she heard a laugh as sensual as Albert's.

"How would it be if you put on something a bit more casual, more relaxed? Would that be a good way to start the night off? There is a silk dressing gown lying in the bedroom. I thought you might like it?"

Tina ran into the bedroom and discovered the dark red dressing gown on the bed. With quick movements she slipped out of her clothes and felt the pleasantly cool silk on her skin. She briefly considered how best to appear in it and came to the conclusion that the greatest joy is in anticipation and so knotted the belt firmly around her waist.

Then she ran barefoot back into the living room, where Albert had already uncorked a bottle of red wine and had even filled the glasses. She would have preferred to take the wine straight into the bedroom, but she was patient and waited to find out what Albert was planning. He grabbed one glass, pressed the other into her hand, lightly clinked them together and took a sip. She did the same. But just as Albert was bending forwards to kiss her their idyll was rudely disturbed. The doorbell tore the two of them out of their intimacy. Albert, gesturing his apologies, put the glass back on the table.

"I'm sorry, darling, but I have to at least see what it is. I am a doctor, you know. After all, it could be an emergency."

Albert opened the front door and Tina could hear him talking softly. The second voice was also masculine, which secretly reassured her. Nothing could be worse than a crazed female patient who had fallen in love with her doctor and turned up out of work hours. Now jealousy began to gnaw at her too. After all, she was not sure of the real nature of her relationship with Albert. What if he fell for one of the many women that he treated daily?

The voices approached and a stranger, who Albert introduced as his good friend, Phil, stepped into the room. Phil gazed knowingly at Tina's short silk dressing gown.

"Oh, I'm disturbing you. Albert, you should have told me. I'll leave again straight away. I only wanted to pop in for a moment. I didn't know you weren't alone."

Tina hurried to play down her state of undress.

"No, no. No problem. Just wait and I'll quickly put something over the top."

Albert and Phil exchanged a brief glance, then Phil nodded and sat himself down on one of the white leather armchairs.

"As far as I'm concerned you can stay the way you are. It seems quite properly dressed to me and looks – if you don't mind me saying – really good, as well."

He smiled at her, making her blush slightly.

"Would you like some wine, too?" offered Albert, and Phil nodded again.

Albert got out a third glass and filled it.

"So, you're the legendary Tina Albert's been talking about nonstop for two weeks? You've completely turned his head."

Tina smiled, partly embarrassed, partly pleased. Even if Albert had not directly said anything to her, she really must have made an impression on him if he had told his friend about her.

"To the start of a truly wonderful three-way friendship," Albert announced rather pompously and raised his glass.

Tina and Phil did the same and Phil added, "Let's drink to the friendship lasting forever!"

Both men emptied their glasses and after a short hesitation Tina did the same. Albert shared out the rest of the wine and looked enquiringly at his girlfriend.

"To Tina," he called out and raised his glass to Phil.

"And you met Albert at Rosi's?" Phil wanted to know.

Tina nodded and tried in vain to formulate a sensible response. What was wrong with her? She had only drunk one glass of wine. Then everything around her went dark and she completely blacked out.

9

Rudolf Schlehmüller only got his name from Blackthorn Mill, 'Schlehenmühle' in German, otherwise he had nothing in common with millers. It was rumoured, in private, that he was the illegitimate son of a rich lord of a manor in the east of the county and that he had inherited his love of music from him. Of course, his father never acknowledged him; that would have been unthinkable. In any case, Rudolf spent his youth along with his mother and older brother on the large estate, and was educated there, together with the legitimate heirs, by a home tutor. Even if he had only felt contempt for his father, he was nevertheless thankful for the opportunity this education gave him, being well aware that, otherwise, he would never have become a music teacher. And when his mother inherited Blackthorn Mill, her parents' house, it was obvious that his older brother would run it. But after Georg's unexpected death at the turn of the century, Rudolf had moved into the mill with his family. He and his wife, Anneliese, took on an apprentice miller who helped her keep the business going while he taught music. This lifestyle arrangement was seen as unconventional and exotic, supplying plenty of fodder to gossipmongers in both the town and the surrounding countryside. On the other hand, when Rudolf realised Margarethe's intelligence and talent, his position pushed open the door to the Girls' High School for her.

Life had been pleasant in Blackthorn Mill until the world war appeared like a spectre in the sky, coming nearer and nearer, its claws hungrily extended for the Schlehmüller family. First it had fetched up Margarethe's oldest brother, Georg, named after his uncle, and after that Horst, only a year younger. Both had been conscripted and, after a short period of training, sent to the front, where they had both been killed. When Rudolf had been called up, the otherwise strong and calm Annaliese had completely broken down. Margarethe would never forget the image of her mother clasping her father's arm, and of him, in tears, tearing himself away from her and running off, off to his death. They had received the bad news just a few days later, and Anneliese had taken to her bed for a week, just lying there and crying. On the eighth day, she had risen early to dress and had worked as usual. From that moment on, Margarethe's father could no longer be mentioned, otherwise her mother would break down again. Margarethe and her two surviving brothers had learnt this lesson quick enough, after making the mistake of mentioning their father in front of their mother just two or three times.

Her father had died in March and in May her brother Klaus disappeared. All they found was a note on his pillow with a short message, telling them he had set off to revenge his father and brothers. Since then, they had heard nothing of him. Only Franz and Margarethe now still lived with their mother in Blackthorn Mill. Nothing else was left of the once happy family. Their apprentice had already long since been called to the front, so that Anneliese and Franz had to try to keep the mill working by themselves. In any case, there was not much to mill anymore because so many fields lay fallow. The farmers and farmhands were all at the front, either injured or killed.

Old Zweistein was one of the few who still possessed a functioning farm, probably because he predominantly employed farm girls instead of farm boys – whatever his motives. One motivation was certainly to lead his son, Albert, back onto the straight and narrow, to give him an appetite for girls. Another was most likely that Frau Zweistein had become a prematurely aged, bitter, and poisonous woman, a woman in whom no one, even with the best will in the world, could find any attractive qualities. Little wonder that old Zweistein found his pleasures elsewhere.

10

When Tina woke up the next morning, she had a dreadful, throbbing headache. Squinting, she opened her eyes and had to think for a moment where she was. Then she heard regular breathing next to her and realised she was lying in Albert's bed. She felt for her phone to find out the time. Damn, already after 8:00. She had never overslept so spectacularly before. She softly pushed the cover aside and slid out of the bed. But didn't Albert have to get up as well? His surgery opened at 8:30. She shook his shoulder lightly and had to smile – he had well and truly taken shelter under the cover.

"Albert, get up. You have to go to work. We've overslept. It's already after 8:00."

But the next moment Tina froze, because, peeling the cover off himself wasn't Albert, but this Phil guy from the night before. Completely shocked, too stunned to say a word, Tina grabbed the bedcover to wrap round herself. Phil opened his eyes, smiled broadly at her and wanted to pull her over to him.

"Now come on, sweetheart. We're not in such a hurry, are we? It sure was nice last night."

These words snapped Tina out of being frozen to the spot. She screamed loudly and quickly gathering her clothes together, fled into the bathroom, where she first locked herself in before collapsing in sobs by the bath. It could only be a bad dream? As much as she racked her brains, she could not for the life of her remember what had happened yesterday. Where the hell was Albert? And how had she ended up in bed next to Phil? Had something really happened? She loved Albert – how could this be possible? Had Phil done something to him? Along with her horror over the situation was now added her concern for her lover. What had actually happened?

She heard Phil on the other side of the bathroom door.

He knocked on it roughly and called out, "Sweetheart, open up – I've still got half an hour."

Oh God – what was she going to do if he kicked the door in? Tina was becoming more and more hysterical.

Shaken by crying fits she yelled, "Get lost, you lousy shithead. Leave."

Astonishingly, nothing happened. He didn't kick the door in, neither did he try the doorknob. He simply said, "Okay," and that was it.

Tina stayed an age locked in the bathroom, listening to her heart beating and slowly calming herself down. She wasn't sure if Phil was still in the house, and so it took half the morning before she finally dared to carefully turn the lock and open the door a crack. Everything was quiet. She slowly came out, gingerly feeling her way step by step from one room to the next. Nothing. Phil had disappeared. But – and that really scared her – there was also no sign of Albert, either. Since she could find no blood, she hoped that he was still alive. On the other hand – perhaps Phil had knocked him out and stuck him in the boot of his car, where by now he would have suffocated, dying miserably. But, surely, wouldn't the girls at his practice have rung by now? She frantically checked the answering machine – no new messages. In her desperation, she decided to check with the surgery. Her fingers trembled as she typed in the number she had, by now, come to know off by heart.

11

Margarethe and Lisette climbed into the waiting carriage. At the front, enthroned on the coach box, sat Albert, who for some mysterious reason had been declared unfit for military service and could therefore continue his studies. What he was studying Margarethe did not know, and she didn't really care. Albert was a strange man. On the one hand she felt herself altogether drawn to him and felt her heart race whenever she saw him, which happened seldom enough. On the other hand, he was also scary. His gaze seemed to slice through people like cold steel, and he gave the impression he was not able to feel any sort of love or attraction for anyone – with the sole exception of Lisette. And when Margarethe heard how the tone of his voice changed from cold as ice to warm as velvet whenever he spoke to Lisette, then she wished he might just for once speak to her like that – she would then die happy.

12

"Dr Zweistein's surgery, Andrea speaking. How may I help you?"

"Hi, it's Tina Hermann. Could I please speak to Dr Zweistein?"

"I'm sorry, he's currently with a patient. What's it about?"

"It's private and really very important. And it will only take a moment – please, can you put me through."

Was it the despair in Tina's voice that did the trick, or was the word 'important' enough? For whatever reason, Tina suddenly heard on-hold piano music and, after a few bars, Albert's dear voice.

"Tina, what is it? I'm in a rush between two patients. Make it short. I have a lot to do."

He was alive. He was healthy. Tina began to cry again, relieved and scared at the same time.

"Albert, what happened yesterday? This Phil guy was alone with me in the apartment. You had gone!"

She avoided saying that he had not only been in the apartment but had also been in bed with her.

"I was so worried when I couldn't find you. I really have no idea what happened yesterday. I'm totally dumbfounded."

Albert laughed coldly. "You're totally dumbfounded? You??? How do you think I'm feeling? Yesterday, without warning, you declare you don't want to have anything more to do with me, that Phil is the cooler guy and that I should just disappear out of your life. I was so shocked and hurt that I left the house and spent the night in my surgery. Look, what the two of you did after that, I really don't care anymore. I mean, how could you do something like that to me? With my best friend? Don't worry, I won't stand in your way, but you need to realise that from now on, I don't want to see or hear from either of you, ever again."

Tina heard a click. Albert had hung up. Tina let her phone drop out of her hand. She was so bowled over by what Albert had just said that she literally went rigid. What had she done? And why? And how come she couldn't remember anything at all?

She was still sitting petrified on Albert's sofa when he came home at lunchtime. It was Wednesday. The surgery shut on Wednesday afternoons.

"What are you still doing here? Just go!" he snarled when he noticed her.

Tina looked up, recognised her fairy-tale prince, jumped up and wanted to throw her arms around him.

"Albert, oh my God, I'm so sorry. I absolutely can't remember anything. It just can't be real. Please forgive me. I have no idea what happened or why. I absolutely can't remember anything."

She let out a desperate sob.

"I still have the image imprinted on my mind, how you threw yourself at Phil. Why should I forgive something like that? So you can do it again at the next opportunity? I'd have to be mad. I really thought you were the right one for me. It's a pity I was fooled like this. And now get out of here!"

He stood by the open living room door like a merciless judge. Tina sprang up and once again tried to throw her arms around her Albert, but he just roughly fended her off, grabbed her by the upper arm and pushed her outside. The front door slammed shut behind her and with that she was shut out of Albert's life. Against her own better judgement, she rang the doorbell insistently a few times, but Albert didn't open up. She hadn't really expected he would. Although she really had no recollection of the previous night, his account of it was more than enough to make it clear she had lost him.

Eventually she set off for home, on foot. It was a beautiful, mild May afternoon, but she didn't notice. She felt neither the warming rays of the sun on her skin, nor heard the chirping of the birds all around her. She didn't see anything: not who she passed, nor who she overtook. She simply didn't register anything at all. She was numb.

At some time or other she arrived back home at her parents', quietly opened the door, and slipped into her room. Her tears had dried up long ago. Her bewilderment at her own behaviour was so great that there was no room left for pain or sorrow. She crept into her bed and almost immediately fell asleep.

She awoke towards evening. For a few seconds she felt happy and lovingly thought of Albert. Then the memory of the ugly scene came back to her, and all that he had said to her pressed down on her like a lead weight. Her phone flashed on, and for a short moment she hoped Albert was ringing her. She hastily unlocked it. Five new messages from Albert – photos. She stared at the images thunderstruck. They were of her and Phil; naked, and explicit.

Below the last photo was written, "You really think I'm going to forgive you?"

13

It certainly wasn't usual for Albert to pick the girls up. It was normally the old stable hand, Wilhelm, known to everyone as Willi, who sat on the coach box, bent double, his stiff leg hanging off to one side. Even Willi considered Margarethe not worth a glance. It was as if she wasn't there. He was in the habit of pulling the horses up for a short moment at the turnoff to Blackthorn Mill so that Margarethe could step down. He had never turned round even once. He would stare straight ahead before making a clicking noise to giddy the horses up in the direction of the Zweistein manor. Albert, on the other hand, on the few occasions he had driven the girls back from school, didn't even think of stopping for Margarethe. He simply kept going, unless, of course, Lisette reminded him. He did everything his sister wanted, so he would then stop at the crossroads. He would presumably never have done that if Margarethe had asked him, but she didn't know that for sure. She had never dared ask.

On that afternoon, like the other times, she prepared herself to walk the extra kilometre. Albert looked even more withdrawn and grim than ever. Margarethe mulled over the reason for his apparent unhappiness. Lisette, however, came straight to the point, which, as his sister, she was naturally allowed to do.

"Albert, what on earth is wrong with you today? You look as if the whole harvest has been ruined by hail. What's got into you?"

Her brother laughed grimly.

"What do you think! And because of it today is supposed to be a day of celebration and dancing. Just imagine, I'm soon to be married. Father has engaged me to Jette, Alfons Bader's daughter. The wedding is planned for next May. I'm engaged to a girl I hardly know and who I certainly wouldn't have chosen myself."

Lisette cried out in disgust and stamped her foot furiously on the coach box, so that the horses nervously tossed their heads and snorted.

Albert tightened his grip on the reins and shouted, "Whoaaa, Aurora! Liesl, what are you up to? Do you want to get us killed?"

So saying, he half turned towards the girls and it was as if, for the first time, he was aware that the invisible Margarethe was on board. He went dark red and then suddenly pale, anxiety written on his face.

"You!" he growled nastily. "You haven't heard anything, understand? If you say just one word, I'll make sure your mother never gets another contract from us and ends up in the poor house. Is that clear?"

Frightened, Margarethe nodded. She could understand Albert well enough because she had a passing acquaintance with Jette Bader herself. Jette was an unpleasant, domineering person, who would never let herself be dominated in return. It was much more likely that Albert Zweistein would have to dance to her tune. Once again, Margarethe could not have known the real reason, that it was precisely because of Jette's character that Albert's father had chosen her as his future daughter-in-law. She would teach his son Albert which way the wind blew.

The rest of the journey went by in silence. Margarethe was plagued by dark thoughts. However interesting she found Lisette's brother at this time in her life, she wouldn't have wanted to change places with Jette for anything. The notion of living with Albert and having to be spoken to like that every day frightened her way too much. On the other hand, she still stubbornly held on to the crazy idea of how it would be if she could make his icy crust melt, if she could get him to use the same tender tone of voice with her that he otherwise reserved for Lisette.

Ah, poor Margarethe! She had no idea that neither she nor Jette could soften this man's heart. Despite all his father's attempts to force it out of him, only a good-looking man named Siegfried set his heart racing, a man he had been meeting in secret for some time.

14

On Friday evening, Phil suddenly appeared at Tina's front door. Of all days, Friday, the very day she had planned to introduce Albert, her fairy-tale prince, to her parents. What had Albert said? 'If we're still together on Friday, then fine.' Had he suspected something would happen? Tina still didn't know what had got into her to treat him the way she had. She had sunk into gloomy despondency, her thoughts circling continuously around Albert, around the dear person she had hurt more than she had ever hurt anyone. In the midst of this gloom, her phone went off. She answered it mechanically. When she recognised the voice of the caller, she wanted to hang up immediately, but his words had already seeped into her consciousness.

"Tina, come out, otherwise I'll keep ringing till your parents come to the door."

For God's sake – that was all she needed!

She answered flatly, "Okay, five minutes."

Actually, it was more like four minutes. By then she had pulled on her tracksuit pants and hoodie, quickly brushed her hair, and opened the front door. Phil stood on the pavement, nonchalantly leaning against a streetlight, and appraised her from head to foot.

"The outfit isn't right. No matter, climb in."

He nodded towards the already old, but well looked-after BMW Z8 that stood at the curb.

"You have to be mad," Tina furiously hissed at him.

Phil just gave a sleazy laugh and waved the envelope he held in his hand.

"You'd be mad if you don't get in. If you don't, your parents will get these beautiful photos of the two of us. Oh, and there's a threesome as well."

Tina suddenly wanted to vomit. She swallowed back the bitter taste and managed to stop herself.

"You're completely crazy. Actually, I don't know what you're talking about," she countered, but it sounded somehow hollow. She still couldn't remember anything of Tuesday night, and that scared her more than she liked to admit.

Her phone went off. A photo. It clearly showed her with Phil and a second man whose head was hidden. She retched again, but somehow managed to keep it down.

"Let's go, get in. I'm not going to say it again."

She was in a total panic about what could happen next, but she had no other choice. She hesitantly walked across the pavement, opened the passenger door, and got in.

Phil lithely slipped into the driver's seat, started the engine, and steered the sports car into the night.

"You're so pretty and such a damn slut," he said to Tina, as he parked the car in front of a modern house on Red Hill. She didn't answer. Her thoughts were racing, but she couldn't grasp anything; no memories, nothing.

"Let's go. Come in with me."

With the same charming nonchalance she associated with Albert, he opened the passenger door for her and helped her out of the car. He then went ahead, opened the front door, and made an exaggerated gesture to motion her into the house.

"What do you want to drink?"

Tina shook her head defiantly.

"Nothing."

"Okay, do as you like. I got in some red wine especially for you. Normally, I only drink white wine. But that's fine."

Tina went on the offensive. She wanted to finally know where she stood.

"What do you actually want?".

Phil gave a sleazy laugh.

"What I want? That's what you're asking? You of all people? After what you pulled off on Tuesday? Albert sure is right to say you'll simply do anything he says. But that sure was over the top."

She froze in terror, feeling utterly helpless because she couldn't remember anything at all. But she tried to hide it as best she could.

"I have no idea what you're talking about. Do you know what I think? I think you want to split Albert and me up using slick photoshopped photos. You're just a shithead."

Phil laughed again and pointed to the sofa.

"Take a seat, madame. Welcome to reality!"

Unwillingly, Tina sat down on the comfortable sofa as far from Phil as possible. A screen rolled down almost soundlessly, and then Phil's movie night began. Tina went as white as chalk as she recognised herself as the female star in an X-rated movie. She was even more shocked by the fact that Albert had lied to her. He had by no means left the house because she had dumped him. Rather, he had spurred her on, participated in everything, filmed everything ... Tina's world crashed in on her, and nothing was as it had been.

When the movie ended, Phil turned round to her with a smug grin on his face.

"Okay, you certainly won't want these scenes played to your parents. And you certainly won't want to see them on the internet, either. So, listen carefully. Here are my conditions. What you so willingly did with the two of us, you will do with me for a year whenever I want, and you will do with every guy I send you to. Don't worry, only respectable clientele, no creeps. After a year, you'll be free to do whatever you like."

15

Astonishingly, Albert stopped at the turnoff of his own accord and let Margarethe step down. Despondent, she said goodbye and trudged up the path to Blackthorn Mill. On the way, she pondered his reasons, whether he had done it to make it less likely she would betray him, or whether her presence had simply disgusted him to the point that he just wanted to get rid of her as quickly as possible.

She sighed. Who would she be able to tell? Her mother perhaps? Her brother, Franz? Laughable. He was happy when he never heard anything about the Zweisteins. Out of necessity, they were dependent on contracts from the manor, but at the human level he didn't want to have anything to do with 'them'.

If he had known of a way to arrange it, he would have personally picked his sister up from school every day. But it wasn't possible. He was needed at the mill and their only horse had been requisitioned by the army some time ago. Only the devil knew how the Zweisteins managed to still have three horses in their stables.

In any case, Franz was less naive than his sister. He had found out why she was able to ride in the carriage. One day, he had arrived home early by accident, when Albert's father was paying his mother one of his visits. Naturally, Franz had slunk off so as not to be noticed. But next day, when Margarethe was at school, he angrily confronted his mother.

She had let herself be insulted without once interrupting, but when he had run out of breath, she asked him just one question that took the wind out of his sails: "Do you want Margarethe to be the one to pay for the carriage fare?"

Since then, Franz hadn't wasted another word on the subject, but had brooded over how he could manage it so Margarethe was no longer reliant on this opportunity for a lift home from school.

16

It wasn't all that long before Tina met up with Albert again. In a professional capacity, so to speak. Of all the humiliations, this was the worst. She had implored Phil not to demand it of her, but Phil had only burst out laughing.

"What are you trying to say?" he had asked. "Albert discovered you. He's certainly got a right to a commission."

Now that Tina was suffering the humiliation of seeing Albert regularly again, it was time for her to let it all come out in the open, to let the videos be made public – how much lower could she sink than she already had? Her parents would cope somehow, and she could drop out of her law degree. Perhaps she could do a baker's apprenticeship. What she had done wouldn't be the kind of disadvantage there that it would be if she tried to become a lawyer or a judge.

But Phil was no idiot – how could she simply presume it could be so easy to get out of it? With a superior smile, he showed her the plans he had made for her so far. Everything from a completely new wardrobe – she certainly couldn't turn up to wealthy clients in a hoodie and tracksuit pants – to the travel costs to Berlin, Amsterdam, Rome, and Paris. Phil had everything neatly listed. Tina's response had been to stare at him in disgust and crumple up the piece of paper.

"Well? What's this got to do with me? You said I have to work for you for a year, otherwise you'll publish the video. All right then, do it. There are worse things."

Phil just laughed. "Naturally there are worse things. You owing me €25,000, for example. With ten percent interest. Pay that back and you can go."

Tina couldn't believe her ears. Was the bastard completely insane?

"You're crazy, Phil. You're not going to get a cent out of me, that was never the deal."

And again, the arrogant grin that made her want to smash his face in.

"Oh yes, my dear, that was a part of the agreement. Look here – you've signed it."

He pulled an agreement for a personal loan out of his briefcase. Tina's signature was clear to see. She went pale.

"Where did you get that?" she whispered, but she already knew the answer.

Naturally, someone who had drunk spiked wine and was as high as a kite would not stop at jumping into bed with strange men; that someone would also sign anything that was shoved in front of her without thinking.

"I hate you Phil. By God, I hate you."

But she hated Albert even more. The man she still loved regardless of what he had done. Tina hadn't known that it was possible to love and hate the same man at the same time. As time passed, every time she met Albert she hoped once more for a miracle, that he would forgive her and buy Phil off, that he would admit what he had done, finally confess his love for her, and make a fresh start with her, this time without lies and deceit, without loaded cards. Then again, she would have loved more than anything to murder Albert for destroying her life. And not only did she hate Albert, she hated herself too, hated herself because, despite everything he had done to her, she still dreamt of a life with him.

"A year, a whole damn year," she had murmured, as he pulled her towards him. And Albert had laughed in her face.

"Tina, dearest, only you believe that. You should have read what you signed more carefully – all travel costs to be charged to your account and, as long as you haven't paid your debts, you'll have to work them off. It says so in black and white."

Albert made another proposal that Tina at first indignantly knocked back. But after thinking about it for some time, she came to the conclusion there was some sense in what he was suggesting.

"How would it be if I gave you something in return, something to make you relax a bit. If you turn up tense to clients, you're sure to get into even more trouble with Phil. Then he will insist you take something before you meet clients – and you certainly won't get the stuff from him for nothing. I mean, I do owe you, in a funny sort of way."

Tina accepted his offer. In a few weeks, when she had got used to working for Phil, perhaps she wouldn't need to take anything anymore. Maybe she could even sell the stuff herself. It was just for a little while …

One thing was clear to Tina – she wouldn't be able to escape from the two of them by legal means. But she would find a way. From that day on she began to search for every little bit of information she could find about Albert and Phil. She would do it. She would find a weak point and pay them back.

17

She had more important things to tell her mother and brother than the news of the stupid wedding – namely, that she was going to be allowed to play piano for the school show.

When she crossed paths with Franz in the yard, it just bubbled out of her.

"Franz, Franz! Would you believe, the 50-year anniversary of the school is in October and they're going to put on a play and guess who's going to do the musical accompaniment, on the school grand piano? Me, me, me!"

With these words she jumped from one leg to the other, which made her look rather childish. Franz brushed away the thought that the Zweistein father could assault this child instead of his mother and smiled at his little sister. Even though he had no great understanding of music, he was genuinely happy for her, for he knew her well enough to know just how much it meant to her.

"Oh, Gretel, that's really lovely for you. Do you already know what you're going to play?"

"Yes, Fräulein Schnittig has already chosen the pieces. 'Liebestraum', for example, you know that one. And she says there will be Wagners there. And the best is, I may, no ... I AM meant to practise every day from now on, on the school piano! I'm going to finally be able to play music again. Franz, I'm so excited!"

"Oh, that really is fantastic, Gretel! Oh, if only dad were here to see it."

For a brief moment, grief settled like a gloomy shadow over Margarethe's joy, but then she said thoughtfully, "Do you know, if there really is a life after death, then he certainly listens to me when I play. And he'll know that I'm playing for him …"

"You're probably right, Gretel. Now run in and tell mother. She'll want to hear about it, too."

While Franz shouldered a sack of wheat and took it to the barn, Margarethe rushed into the house to look for her mother.

Naturally enough, Rudolf's widow was also glad to hear the news. She was convinced that it would do her daughter good to finally be able to play the piano again.

She reflected that even if Margarethe had thought differently about it, it would have been anything but easy for her to sell the piano. She knew how much it had meant to Rudolf. It was the one thing he had ever been given by his father. He had accepted the gift even though he had felt nothing but contempt for the old man, who had called him a bastard and hounded his mother from the estate because his legal wife could no longer bear the sight of the boy who looked the spitting image of his father.

Yes, he had taken the piano because his love of music had far outweighed his hatred of his father and because, as a clever young man, he had seen in the gift a chance to achieve something that he could never have achieved without it.

No, it had been everything other than simple to part with the piano. And Margarethe and Franz had no idea that it now resided on Rudolf's father's estate, in the hope he would one day bequeath it to Margarethe.

Margarethe ran light-footed up the stairs to her room after first getting a promise from her mother to go to the show. She started her homework but couldn't concentrate, and when she heard her mother call out to Franz down in the yard, she quickly sprang up and kneeled on the floorboards. She carefully freed a loose board and felt about in the opening with one hand. Having located what she was looking for, she drew out a package wrapped in brown paper and opened it almost devoutly. Inside were sheets of music, carefully arranged. No one else knew anything about them, neither her mother nor her brother. She would take them to school the next day and she would practise the piece when she could be sure everyone had gone home, and she was alone in the school.

18

A stroke of luck came to Tina's aid, a stroke of luck named Dr Held. She stumbled across Phil's name in a file in Dr Held's chambers.

The file, all meticulously written down in longhand by Frau Mauser, contained everything worth knowing about the mysterious 2012 fire that completely destroyed the Crystal Spa resort in Fichtelberg, 30 kilometres to the east of Bayreuth. Everything was in there about the subsequent legal battle over the sum insured and the wrangling over a possible new project on the site.

And Phil was mixed up in it; Tina was absolutely sure of that. He was not simply what he seemed in the records, the advertising partner of Steinhart, the owner. He had to have known things that were not in the files. The longer and more intensively she delved into the case, the more unavoidable this crazy suspicion became that Phil was somehow mixed up in the whole affair. Of course, Tina knew the official files themselves would not reveal anything. But the suspicion had become an obsession. She only needed proof …

Like a bloodhound she set about following Phil's scent and researched the records of the Municipality of Fichtelberg and there found out that Albert had apparently taken an interest in the vacant site where the spa resort had stood. In the end, the purchase had been prevented by the long-running dispute concerning the sum insured.

Albert? How deeply was he involved? Right at the beginning of their relationship he had mentioned to Tina that he would like to build a beauty clinic. Had he planned to do it in Fichtelberg?

Tina again mulled over the spa resort story. Was there really something in it? But why and how was Phil connected? She sensed that if there was really something to it and she could find it out, she would then have the two bastards in the palm of her hand. And if she had something on them, she would be able to free herself from their clutches.

So, she poked about in the files at every opportunity, clinging persistently to this thin thread of hope. At the same time, she ostentatiously took the trouble to maintain good relations with Phil and Albert – the more normal and at ease she was with them, the more they would become careless and give something away. That, at least, was what she hoped. And with time her efforts did begin to prove successful – a careless offhand remark here, an overheard telephone conversation there. The portrait of the two crooks was getting ever more detailed and precise.

Tina tirelessly researched all matters relating to the Crystal Spa. She used every unobserved minute to search in Dr Held's files, but without success. Whatever had happened at the spa resort, apparently it hadn't been arson, because the insurance broker had paid up after a tough legal battle. So that was a dead-end, despite her gut feeling.

Tina was disappointed, but she didn't give up. If it hadn't been Fichtelberg, then there was certainly some other shady project of Albert and Phil's waiting for her to discover. She doggedly investigated how the friendship between the two men had actually begun. Where did they know each other from? What business connections were they maintaining or had already cultivated in the past?

She knew that sometime in the not-too-distant future she would find decisive proof. And then she would have no scruples. She wouldn't shy away from blackmailing the two of them. She knew she would have to fight to be free of them – with gloves off. She wanted to be well-armed when it got that far.

Phil with his mansion in Bayreuth, his fashion house in Milan, his hundreds of connections in the fashion and advertising industries – she would be able to blow all that up quickly. But that would not ruin him permanently. He would only laugh and exploit her even more. No, she didn't have enough on him yet. She had to find something that would well and truly bring him undone as soon as it became known. And she sensed that the key to her freedom was somehow buried in the affair of the spa resort.

And Albert? Albert with his beautiful estate in Wolfsbach, his stylishly furnished living room, his heavenly bedroom and – not forgetting – his oh so fabulous drawing room housing his uncle's grand piano? Everything, he would lose everything – if, that is, he didn't want to enjoy it together with her! She wanted to make him grovel. She wanted to make him come snivelling to her, beg her like she had begged him.

Tina imagined what it would be like to have so much power over Albert that his destiny lay in her hands. She kept imagining giving him the finishing blow, kicking him one last time before she returned to her own life. Or else, how would it be if she let herself soften when confronted by his grovelling, sparing him in return for marrying her?

But no, why should she? So that he could look for an opportunity to avenge himself on her, just like she was going to avenge herself on him? Too uncertain, too dangerous. Especially since a doctor had so many more options than your average man in the street to bring about the death of a loved one. She felt that she almost had him in the palm of her hand. All that was missing was solid evidence.

It was, after all, more than curious that Albert's farmland, already zoned as a protected environmentally sensitive area, should have suddenly become rezoned for housing at the same time that his building application in Fichtelberg was rejected. Too many coincidences all at the same time for Tina's liking. Then there was the telephone conversation that Tina had overheard. She had not learned much, but it was altogether conceivable that Albert had someone in the building authority he was bribing.

Whatever the truth might be, she had to stick at it. Everyone had their weak spot. That had become clear to her after that fateful night. It only depended on being tenacious and sharp enough to uncover the weak spots of Phil and Albert.

19

In the evening, when her eyes had already closed, Margarethe let her thoughts scurry about like little mice, and quite on their own they scurried back to the night when her parents had argued so terribly. The loud voices had woken Margarethe. She had had no idea what it was actually about, but her mother had been beside herself.

"Have you gone completely mad? Running off with this music! How can you be so stupid? Don't you realise you'll be the first person they'll suspect? They'll notice it's missing and then you'll be in for it. You'll never get another position anywhere if you've been in prison. Or, even worse, as an ex-prisoner, you'll be first in line to be sent to the front. How can you do something like this to us?"

Then the calmer voice of her father.

"Annie, calm down! I'm sure they won't tell the police. It's something the old man will want swept under the carpet, and the son just as much. Perhaps he's hidden the music from his father so that he doesn't find out about his appalling affair. Because I'm certain about one thing: the dear boy loves ..."

At this point her father's voice sank, so that Margarethe could not understand the rest of the sentence. But soon he spoke again at his previous level.

"Then again, the reason might be that he's planning to do something with the music that makes it vital that the actual composer doesn't become known. I have no idea what that

something might be. Perhaps that person doesn't want to be associated with the piece. Perhaps the boy wants to claim all the glory for himself. There must be some reason for the music being hidden in the piano. And so long as I have the music, presumably I can make good use of it."

What music? And which boy? Margarethe wracked her brains. Perhaps one of her brothers? No, they weren't in the least interested in music. And besides, her father had spoken about an old man, and he wouldn't call himself that. The whole thing was weird. She couldn't make any sense of it.

She had not heard what her mother had said in reply, only noticing the complaining tone of voice. But soon, concentrating on the argument, she made out her mother once more.

"You must promise me – this music will be the ruin of all of us. If you still have a spark of love for me, then destroy it. I'm imploring you, do it! If not for me, then for our children. It's simply not worth it, believe me."

And her father replied unwillingly, "For heaven's sake, if you want me to do it so much, then I'll do it. Still, I can't understand you. It gives us a chance to finally get a piece of the cake. And you want to give it up just because you're afraid of something that won't happen. But all right, I'll do it. Only don't complain anymore that we don't have enough money."

Doors slammed, then all Margarethe could hear was her mother softly crying. Her father must have gone out to burn the music or bury it in the dung heap.

20

Tina seethed inside. Another one of these senseless evenings, frittered away with the man she loved and hated and with the man she only hated. Albert and Phil were sitting in the living room while she had been sent into the kitchen like a servant. There again, considered soberly, that was all she was. Phil sent her to his business partners in half of Europe, and when he hadn't made any appointments for her, then she had to be there for him and Albert. In a fury, she let the dishes clatter as she put them back in the cupboard. Phil promptly yelled out that she should stop making so much noise and instead come and sit with them.

Not even as good as a servant! She knew only too well how these evenings ended, and she was fed up with it.

Unwillingly, she went into the living room where the two men had uncorked a bottle of champagne.

"Go on, get yourself a glass, sweetheart. We've got something to celebrate."

Albert toasted her a little tipsily. Every part of her being balked at doing what she was told, but good sense won out. It would only have caused an argument if she had refused the champagne, and if she was lucky, she might even hear a few worthwhile details. So, she fetched a third glass out of the cupboard and let Phil fill it.

"What are you celebrating, then?" she asked as casually as possible.

Phil only brushed the question aside and mumbled something to himself, but Albert was apparently in a triumphant mood that made him talkative.

"The land that belongs to our estate in Wolfsbach, can you remember me mentioning it? It's supposed to become a nature conservation reserve. Haven't you said something about a girlfriend of yours who's campaigning for it? On account of some frogs?"

"Toads. European spadefoot toads.," Tina informed him without thinking. "My friend from school, Marie-Claire, she's totally committed to it. She's just told me that the application is as good as submitted to the Environment Protection Authority. Has it actually been approved? You'd certainly get compensation, if that's the case. Can you make a good profit from that?"

Albert laughed.

"Profit? From a nature conservation area? You must be dreaming. There's no profit in that. But I've been lucky. It's much better than that. The land isn't going to become a conservation reserve, it's going to become a new housing estate, just like Storchennest. In fact, the entire development is going to be called Storchennest II. It's going to be a family-friendly development. And instead of €50 a square metre, I'm going to get a cool €110. We submitted the application to the construction authority today. If that's not a reason to celebrate, then I don't know what is. Cheers!"

Tina forced herself to smile in delight.

"I'm so happy for you, Albert. It sounds like a really lucrative deal. Are you selling to the council? How does it work?"

The two men grinned at each other, and Albert explained his plan.

"First the application has to be examined and that will take about another year. But I'm certain that everything will work out. I'll then have to sell two thirds of the land to the council, for €110 a square metre. The remainder I'll have to sell within a specified time limit for a maximum of €135, otherwise it reverts to the City of Bayreuth for €110. But Phil will buy the remainder from me. He has the necessary small change, and then we can speculate with the land as much as we want. Two, three years waiting time, and then we'll make a killing. Brilliant, isn't it?"

He emptied his glass in one swig and refilled it. It didn't worry him in the least that he spilt half of it over himself.

"And then we can finally build the beauty clinic on Eierberg, in Saas, near my estate in Wolfsbach. My grandparents had wanted to sell off our land for housing I don't know how many years ago, but then the war got in the way. It sure is a great feeling to finish an old family project."

Albert grinned a bit stupidly. It was all too apparent that he had over-celebrated the deal. Phil, on the other hand, just frowned.

"You mustn't blab on to Tina like this. Don't you know her pretty little head can't process so many figures? Besides, we still haven't negotiated with the owner of the Eierberg. So don't count your chickens just yet."

He flashed a menacing glance at Albert, making it obvious to Tina that he wanted him to shut up. A pity she wouldn't hear anything more, but she had heard enough to know the two of them were up to something shady. Now she just needed to be skilful in using the knowledge. Tina wanted to see Albert as much as Phil brought down.

21

Only a few days later her father had received his call-up papers. It seemed to Margarethe that it was only yesterday that she had come home from school to a gloomy, frightening house. The mill had stopped – that had just about never happened before. She had not seen or heard her brothers Klaus or Franz outside. The chimney had been cold and smokeless, although winter had been far from over and, after a short thaw, everything had again been covered by a thin layer of wet snow. Margarethe remembered the feeling of dread, her heart racing, her head throbbing.

Hesitantly, she had opened the front door and stepped into the house. Everyone had been assembled in the kitchen – her parents, her brothers. There had been no food on the table. Her father and her brothers had had faces as white as chalk. Her mother had been crying into her apron. Margarethe had asked in confusion what had happened.

It had been Franz who had softly answered, "Father has to go to the front. The day after tomorrow …"

Forgetting her hunger, not worrying that she was freezing, she had thrown herself into her father's arms, had cried like a little child, but had found no consolation there. However, in the evening – her mother was still sitting in the kitchen as if drugged – her father had motioned her outside and had gone into the dark barn with her.

"Margarethe, can you keep a secret?" he had asked her softly.

Unnerved, she had nodded. What had he wanted to say to her that the others had not been allowed to hear?

"What's it about?" she had wanted to know.

"Margarethe, it's very important that you don't tell anyone about our talk, and that no one sees what I'm going to pass over to you. I've got something here that your mother thinks I no longer have. I would like you to keep it in a safe place for me until I come back – because I will come back, I promise you that. You can simply leave it hidden here, but I want you to know about it. Come and look!"

In the furthest corner of the barn he had grabbed hold of a split floorboard and fetched out a package, wrapped in thick brown paper. Before he had even opened it, Margarethe knew it contained the pages of sheet music she had heard her parents arguing about so fiercely. Stunned, she had taken the first page, studied the handwritten lines of music and had let the melody touch her. She had been seized by a mysterious spell that had been difficult to shake off.

"So, you haven't destroyed them," she said tonelessly. "But you promised mother. Why are they so important to you, more important than us?"

Her father had gone pale.

"You overheard our argument?"

He had sounded cross.

"I wasn't being sneaky. You were so loud that I couldn't help waking up and hearing that you were arguing about some pages of sheet music. But what is it about them that's so important to you?" Margarethe had insisted.

"That doesn't matter, child. What's important is that nothing happens to them, and nobody finds them. Do you know they're very valuable? Handled in the right way they can be worth a small fortune and for that reason alone it's

worth keeping them. You have to promise me to keep a good eye on them and not to tell your mother you have them. You mustn't tell anyone you have them. They're so valuable that it would be worth committing a crime to get hold of them. So be careful. It's just till I'm back home. The war won't last forever, and I'll take care of myself. As soon as I'm back here again, I'll look after them again and make some money out of them. Agreed?"

How could she refuse her father his parting wish? Naturally, she had promised him everything he wanted.

When he had left home two days later, the pages of sheet music had been forgotten. Her brothers had stood deathly pale at the front door. She had cried and embraced her father for the last time. As he had gone to leave, her mother had rushed after him, clung to his arm, clasped him, and screamed, cried, raged that he shouldn't go away, that he had to stay with her. Her father had cried too, tears streaming down his cheeks, leaving behind wet traces, like snail trails on wet earth. It was not right. It was not proper. Men shouldn't have to cry. Margarethe had realised this at that moment without consciously thinking it. Finally, with a loud sob he had torn himself away from her mother and run off. That had been the last time she had seen him alive, or dead, for that matter, for he had been hastily buried in foreign soil.

While her mother had kept crying from morning to night, Margarethe had gone around in a daze. March and April had been lifeless, dead months. May had swept over the land and had gone again, and with it, Klaus, disappearing out of their lives forever. He had crept away in the dead of night. When, early in the morning, he had not come down for breakfast, Margarethe had been sent upstairs to wake him and check if he was sick. She had not found him but only a hastily written note, which lay on his pillow.

"Dear mother, Margarethe, and Franz," he had written. "Don't be sad or angry, but I have to leave. Someone has to avenge my father and my brothers. And who is that going to be if not me? I will fight for them. I will make amends for what was done to them. I'll come back when the war is over, and the enemy beaten. Until then, don't forget me and carry me in your hearts. Your Klaus."

Again she had cried and again her mother had been unapproachable for days on end. After that Klaus could not be mentioned, no more than his father or his missing brothers.

22

Marie-Claire was sitting comfortably cross-legged on the big bed in Tina's room. Her appearance did not go with her French name at all, a name which promised aristocracy, and created expectations of an elfin-like creature with bisque porcelain skin. The real-life Marie-Claire was quite the opposite: stocky, tanned, with short thin hair and always dressed in overalls and gumboots – or espadrilles in dry weather. Most of the time she carried around an old bucket and a butterfly net and she was almost always holed up in her tiny student digs with several animal foundlings that needed to be coddled. Even today she was carrying one around in the bib pocket of her faded overalls, a small dwarf bat with an injured wing that had crept in there and only peeped out now and again to beg with shrill nagging for the mealworms Marie-Claire readily shoved between its needle-sharp teeth.

"It can only be a question of a few days, perhaps one, or at the most, two weeks before the spadefoot toads in Wolfsbach will be safe, as well as the rare habitat of the broad-leafed orchid. It's amazing – until recently nobody knew this variety even occurred in the Bayreuth basin, let alone so many of them. We absolutely have to intervene to protect them. This Zweistein guy, who owns the meadowland, he's leased the lot to some farmers who don't seem to care at all. They throw their manure around without considering what threatened plants might be lost. It takes years for orchids to grow again on land that has been over-fertilised."

Marie-Claire shoved another mealworm into the snout of her tiny tot and drank a big mouthful of tea. Tina sat opposite her on the office chair and stared hypnotised at the bat until its head again disappeared into the bib pocket.

"And what if it shits all over you?" she asked, visibly horrified, but her old school friend only laughed.

"And? Firstly, bat droppings are a great fertiliser. I can shake them out and spread them over a bed of tomatoes. Secondly, you can wash clothes. They don't have to be new, do they?"

Tina was unconvinced and far from thrilled by the uninvited guest that was now beginning to chirp softly.

"Don't let it out, do you hear?"

"Don't panic. Anyway, Edward can't fly at the moment, and as long as it is still light, he won't get restless."

"Edward?"

"Yeah, he has to have a name. Why not Edward?"

Marie-Claire laughed again. It was a bell-like laugh that you wouldn't expect from the look of her.

"Listen, I have to tell you something – but don't lose your temper, OK?" Tina began.

Her friend was distracted by a fleeing mealworm that had escaped out of the food box onto the bedcover and was being hastily put back.

"Don't let any maggots into the bed, I warning you – otherwise we're not going to be friends for very long."

"Aw, come on. They're not maggots, they're mealworms. And they won't hurt you, even if they should manage to crawl under your cover. They'll pupate and as soon as they become mealworm beetles, they'll whizz into the kitchen to find something to eat. So don't panic."

Remembering that Tina had begun to speak, she asked, "What were you wanting to say?"

Tina sighed. It was not going to be easy for her to disappoint her friend, but she had to. She was sure of one thing – if anyone could put a stop to the underworld activities of Albert and Phil, it was Marie-Claire.

"Look, Marie-Claire – the conservation area is not going to happen. The land will be rezoned as a housing development and Storchennest II will be built there. Say goodbye to your orchids, no matter whether they're green, yellow, or red, and ciao to your spadefoot toads. Albert Zweistein is going to make a pretty penny out of it and his friend Phil Großmann as well. It's all done and dusted and if you don't believe me, I know about it first-hand."

Marie-Claire went pale, jumped up and spilt mealworms all over the bedcover. As Tina grabbed a sheet of cardboard and busily shovelled the creepy-crawlies back into their box, the biology student gasped indignantly for air.

"And what do you mean by first-hand?" she asked flatly. Tina sighed and grimaced.

"Albert Zweistein is first-hand. I am a good friend of both him and Phil Großmann and that's why they've kept me in the loop."

"What?"

Now Marie-Claire went properly through the roof.

"You're a good friend of both of them? And you haven't talked them out of it? And you know very well how important it is to protect this habitat! And how have they managed to have it rezoned, when an application by the Environment Protection Authority has been known for ages? How can you go along with them?!"

"Marie … that's not how it is … what could I have done to stop them? They don't listen to me. Money is more important to them than doing the right thing. Believe me, I can't change anything or influence them. You have to understand that. And what does it really matter – it's only a few toads and perhaps a hundred orchids. Other places and other animals and plants are destroyed for a lot less than Albert and Phil are going to make."

"Tina! How can you say that? In fact, I expect you to help me confront these guys as soon as possible. What's more, I expect you to back me up when I shoot their arguments to pieces."

So, it all came down to this. What Marie-Claire had in mind would not lead to anything but would only pit her against Phil. He could absolutely not tolerate loose talk. In Tina's mind there was no question about it, she must protect herself.

"You can't be serious, Tina. If that's really your opinion, then we're no longer friends."

Tina shrugged her shoulders.

"I'm sorry, but nothing can be done."

Marie-Claire stared furiously at Tina and Tina stared back, the two girls finishing up looking daggers at each other. After a few seconds, Tina looked away and Marie-Claire rushed out. The front door slammed, and a single mealworm fell off the bedcover onto the floor, creeping unnoticed under the carpet.

Tina Hermann began to cry.

After what felt like an eternity she reached for her laptop and started a search. If she delved deeply enough, then perhaps she would learn something about the sinister beauty clinic on the Eierberg in Sass. All she knew for now was that no land had yet been released for development there. But Tina was certain that what Phil and Albert were planning in Wolfsbach would also succeed in Saas with their plans for the Eierberg. She would have loved to know how the two of them had managed to even have their application discussed. Had they bribed someone in the building authority? Or in the Environment Protection Authority? Or even someone further up? Tina was not sure. The murky contacts of her pimps reached into swamps of corruption she could not even imagine.

After a long search she found an ancient newspaper article that actually mentioned the planning for a clinic on the Eierberg that had been put on ice because of fears about the effects on the adjoining protected wetland. Was Albert really wanting to go through with it now? Tina decided she would personally visit the Eierberg as soon as she had time. She remembered that a friend had once casually mentioned that she was stabling a horse there. Perhaps it was time to come and visit the old nag.

A soft ping alerted her to an incoming message – from Marie-Claire. Tina opened it apprehensively.

"You'll regret this!!!"

Well, certainly not backing down – more like a declaration of war. With a sigh she moved the email to the trash and closed her laptop.

23

That was the May that was followed by an unusually warm June. Once again, Margarethe thought of her father's legacy. What was she supposed to do with it? Eventually she loosened a floorboard in her bedroom and hid the pages of sheet music there. After several days of gloomy indecision, she decided to go and ask her mother what that last argument had been about – naturally without confessing that the music had not been destroyed.

She waited for an afternoon when Franz was out of the house. She crept anxiously into the kitchen, where her mother was standing at the stove making strawberry jam out of the few tiny strawberries that the barren garden still produced. Margarethe grabbed a tea towel and dried the hot rinsed jars. She searched for the right words.

"Mother … you and father woke me up when you were arguing about some sort of music. You said it would be the ruin of us all, and father eventually said he would destroy it. What was so terrible about it?"

When she asked, she did not look up, did not dare make eye contact with her mother.

The proprietress of Blackthorn Mill did not answer immediately, so that Margarethe at first thought that she had not heard her. But then abruptly all hell broke loose, making Margarethe cringe.

"How can you dare ask that? Your father was my greatest love. We never ever argued about anything. Whatever you think you heard must have been in a dream. There wasn't any music. We never fell out. And only this cursed war has been the ruin of us all!"

The wooden cooking spoon was plunged into the saucepan with so much force that the hot strawberry jam splattered all over the place, some landing on Margarethe's bare arm.

The sudden pain made Margarethe scream, but her mother did not hear. She had turned on her heel and run sobbing out of the kitchen. Margarethe stared after her in astonishment, but then practical thoughts won her over and she took care of the abandoned jam so that it could at least still be used to sweeten their meagre meals. She even let herself eat a whole spoonful on the sly. But it could not console her in any way, as she had by no means learned anything new about the mysterious pages of sheet music.

Since now, in summer, the evenings were longer, and the mornings were bright earlier, Margarethe could examine the pages of sheet music in her bedroom without anyone noticing. In winter her mother would have become suspicious when the candles were used up more quickly than normal, but now nobody noticed Margarethe bringing the music out and studying it almost daily. She would sit on her bed, let her index finger glide over the lines, and hum the notes silently to herself.

She would have loved to just once been able to play the piece on a piano. She would have loved to actually hear it. However, that had become impossible. Since her father's death her mother had, much to Margarethe's vexation, sold the piano. So, all she had left was to conjure up the chords and passages in her mind and note where to play softly and where to play loudly. Her fingers twitched on her thigh and played imaginary notes, but that was all the practice she could do.

And sometimes, when Margarethe was in an especially dreamy mood, she puzzled over the mysterious dedication, which was written to the right of the title on the first page: 'For my Beloved A. From S.W. in Everlasting Remembrance'. Who on earth was A.? Perhaps it was Albert Zweistein, Lisette's brother, the mysterious, the unapproachable Albert. And who was S.W.? Sieglinde? Sabine? Susanne? However much Margarethe mulled over it, she could think of no girls she knew with those initials. And, if she was honest, the writing did not look like it had been done by a girl. A man's then? The father or the grandfather of the mysterious A? An uncle, perhaps? Margarethe's imagination could not go further than that, but the handwriting did not fit her guesswork. It looked too young, too lively. Mysteries on top of mysteries were connected to this music.

When the day eventually arrived for the audition for the school play and Margarethe got the offer to play the musical accompaniment, there was an additional benefit – she would finally be able to actually play the piece. She just had to be careful to make sure she was alone in the school when she practised it. The words of her father, that nobody should find out that the pages of sheet music existed, had made a deep impression on her. Then again, it would surely not pose a problem, because the music teacher was certainly not going to hang about at the school after classes for hours on end on account of just one student. As was usual in such cases, Margarethe would be given a key, on condition that she locked up when she left.

24

"Tina! Tina? Are you home?"

An overexcited Anna called out so loudly she could be heard across half the house. Tina came out of her room fuming. She had been enjoying a rare, peaceful evening off from Phil, only to now have it shattered by her little sister screaming the house down.

"Yes, for hell's sake – what is it? Stop screaming like that."

"Hell, you're in a bitchy mood again, aren't you? Anyway, Frau Grimm wants to know if you can clean our costumes. We've found some old skirts and blouses that are ancient. We want to wear them in the anniversary production, but they have to be cleaned first. They're too delicate to be stuffed into a washing machine. Can you get them dry-cleaned?"

Despite making plenty of money for Phil, Anna did not get to see any of it, apart from what was spent on clothes and accessories, so she still had to keep up her part-time jobs, like working for the local dry cleaner.

Tina found it almost fascinating how unaffected Anna was by her bad mood. Then again, she herself had happy memories of participating in Frau Grimm's theatre group productions. The recollection briefly banished her dark mood, so much so that she heard herself naturally agreeing to the request. Anna smiled back at her happily.

"Great, but I knew straightaway you'd do it. So, I've got the things here with me. Look, here they are in the bag."

She pointed to the big travel bag on wheels in the hallway. Her curiosity peaked, Tina opened the zip and rummaged inside. Her nostrils were assaulted by musty air from the previous century. She pulled out a heavy dark-blue woollen skirt.

"Ah, yuck – do you really want to put something like this on? What are you performing? Some tragedy from before World War I? Effi Briest, perhaps?"

Tina was genuinely horrified by the musty old-fashioned clothes, but Anna only laughed.

"No, the play is called 'Dance of the Elves' and is as old as the clothes. You absolutely have to come to the performance, it's not long to go now. Oh yeah, we'll give your boss a big thank you. The dry cleaning will naturally be mentioned in the programme credits – if he gives us a discount, that is."

"Well, I think you'll need to ask him about that yourself, but I'm sure it'll be all right. Go on, give me the grubby old things. I'll actually be working there tomorrow. I'll look after them then."

Tina closed the bag and wheeled it into the garage. No way did she want the mouldy things spending the night in her bedroom. Actually, she could look through everything right away if she already had hold of them. Without hesitation she tipped the contents onto the floor, put the open travel bag in the boot of her ancient, dented Opel Corsa, and picked each piece of clothing up individually so she could check the pockets before repacking it.

There were just a few skirts left on the ground when Tina suddenly stopped short. What was that? Had the inside of the pocket been torn. Why did nothing stop her from reaching in so deeply. No, it was no ordinary opening because she could hear something rustling. She reached in deeper, and her fingers felt paper. Tina carefully pulled the sheet out and stared at it.

It had yellowed after many years tucked away undisturbed. It looked like a prop from an old movie, but you could still see that it was a page of sheet music written in black ink. The title was simply 'Sonata', inscribed above the lines of music.

More interesting was the annotation that was written in almost lovingly drawn letters on a slant in the upper right corner. Once Tina had deciphered the spidery handwriting a contented smile spread over her face. She had just found the missing piece of the puzzle she needed to finish to free herself from Phil, because it was a dedication that was written in the corner: 'For my Beloved A. from S.W. in Everlasting Remembrance'. And if she wasn't completely mistaken, this was the exact proof Dr Held had demanded from his client to be able to sue the Zweisteins.

25

Rudolf ran over the open field that lay between Blackthorn Mill and the road to Bayreuth. An ice-cold wind whistled round his ears, and he shivered as he rubbed his hands together. His simple rabbit fur mittens warmed his hands a bit, but in temperatures that were in the double digits below zero, and on a bright, sunny day, they were nowhere near warm enough. The low February sun did not have enough strength to blind him, but the light glaring off the snow did. All things considered, it was not a day to stay out in the open any longer than necessary.

Despite that, Rudolf had to make his way along the route to the Zweistein estate to give Lisette her obligatory piano lesson. He was well aware that he would not be able to move his fingers properly in the first half hour of the lesson and so would not be able to play anything for her. If he had not been so utterly dependent on the money, he would have thrown the music in the elder Zweistein's face long ago.

How could a man treat his son in such an unfeeling and domineering way? How could he take his cherished piano playing away from him and force him to do shooting practice instead? Rudolf asked himself how often it happened that families treated each other like this, parents their sons, husbands their wives. Surely it would have been simpler for everyone concerned not to compel Albert to do something that obviously left him feeling shattered.

Of course, it was none of his business. It was not his child. Nevertheless, it made him furious. He had liked teaching Albert. Albert had been a keen and interested student. Lisette was, on the other hand, nothing like her brother. Lisette was nothing more than the spoilt daughter of the lord of the manor without much up top and lamentably lacking even a shred of feeling for music. She was not diligent at practice; it bored her. She was a pretty face with nothing behind it. But it was money. It was food on the table. So, Rudolf had to make the most of it and regularly run off to the manor house, often in the icy cold like today, to teach this clueless girl.

At least he got a cup of weak tea to warm him up when he entered the drawing room. Today there were no members of the Zweistein family around but after about five minutes an ill-tempered Lisette came in. She made it all too clear that she got no joy out of piano lessons. A maid servant waved a feather duster around the walls, probably so that the daughter of the house was not left alone with a man. Lisette unwillingly opened up the keyboard and began to play haltingly. It was obvious that she had not practised, and Rudolf wrinkled his brow in annoyance.

"Lisette, you have to spend more time practising. Half an hour daily is the minimum if you want to improve."

It was not the first time he had stressed the need for practice. And not for the first time she replied impertinently, "Who says I want to?"

But she played on nevertheless, tried to play a quick passage at full speed, despaired of it and got stuck at the same spot again and again. Rudolf let out an audible snort of derision. In the meantime, his fingers had warmed up and so he interrupted his pupil to show her how to play the phrase by playing it himself. But at the highest note in the passage he stopped, annoyed because the note did not sound. Something seemed to be caught in the piano. Perhaps something was wrong with one of the felt-covered hammers that struck the strings to make the note.

He tried it once more and then a third time just to make sure, before saying, half to Lisette, half to the maid servant, "Something's not right – I'll have to take a look inside the piano."

Lisette shrugged her shoulders and declared that she would take a break for a few minutes. The feather duster waving maid servant, considering her task over, also left the drawing room.

Rudolf stared at the closed door for a moment before, shaking his head in irritation, he set about investigating the insides of the piano. Just one glance was enough to discover the cause. A few sheets of paper were stuck in the piano, carefully rolled up together so that they would not get in the way of the action and as a result be discovered. Nevertheless, one sheet had come loose and rolled itself up again, a corner becoming wedged under the hammer and so blocking it from hitting the strings.

Rudolf drew this sheet out and examined it with suppressed curiosity. At first, he had expected to find a love letter or a page out of a diary hidden there by Lisette. But then it dawned on him that if that had been the case, she would certainly not have left the drawing room but would have done everything in her power to prevent it being found.

After he had smoothed out the page and held it to the light, he saw that it was a piece of sheet music. There was a dedication on it: 'For my Beloved A. from S.W. in Everlasting Remembrance'. Rudolf pondered who the initials could stand for. A. stood for Albert, that was certain. And S.W. was, judging by the writing, just as certainly not a woman, but a mysterious lover of Albert's. That was why the sheets were hidden here – no one should find them.

Rudolf looked around quickly. Neither the maid servant nor Lisette had returned, all doors were closed and there was nobody to be seen outside the windows. In just a few seconds Rudolf made his momentous decision. He drew the roll with the rest of the pages out of the body of the piano and untied the already dislodged string that had held the sheets together. He quickly smoothed them out, laid the loose page on top and let them all disappear into his calf leather briefcase beside the pieces he had brought along with him. Now all he had to do was finish the piano lesson and leave the estate without attracting attention.

Rudolf was convinced that if he just disappeared with the pages of sheet music nothing more would happen. Albert had hidden them there so no one – and above all not his father – would ever find them. To pursue Rudolf or take legal action against him would have meant that the business would be broadcast far and wide. Albert could not allow that. No. As soon as Rudolf had hidden the pages, he would be safe and would have a means of pressuring Albert to ensure his family got through the war without hunger …

Lisette, now called back, was not overjoyed that the piano had been repaired so quickly. What Rudolf told her about a piano hammer that had supposedly been unseated did not interest her in the least. Unengaged, she tinkled her way through the rest of the time and jumped up relieved and without a thank you when the grandfather clock announced the end of the lesson. In other circumstances, Rudolf would have gazed at his retreating pupil with a shake of his head, but today he hurried out of the house.

He ploughed his way through the snow-covered ground back to Blackthorn Mill with long rapid strides, his briefcase firmly clasped under his arm. He did not feel the biting cold on the way back. On the contrary, the stolen goods were almost too hot to handle. Rudolf had never committed a crime before, and accordingly felt bad about it. As he made his way home, his conscience began to torment him cruelly and only the thought of his hungry family prevented him from turning round on the spot and putting the pages of sheet music back in their hiding place.

26

With a quick glance in all directions, the dark hooded figure stepped out of hiding. Just a few hurried steps, another glance all round, a quick grab in the water. Orderly, inconspicuous retreat. Triumphant grin. That had been a complete success.

27

"Three-quarters two!" said Lotte, deliberately speaking as broadly as possible in her native Upper Franconian dialect so that the words only sounded vaguely like normal German. Germans in general would say 'half two' for 'half past one', but Doris had never heard of the expression 'three-quarters two' before.

Doris tried to imitate Lotte but only succeeded in pronouncing 'two' the way Lotte had said it.

Lotte was sitting on the desk and trying in vain to explain to her new colleague from Cologne how to say the time the right way, the Upper Franconian way. Cologne was a long way from Bayreuth and before she arrived Doris had never encountered a dialect so different from normal German before.

Lotte's latest attempt to teach Doris how to speak properly and tell the time in the right way had begun with a harmless enquiry.

"Doris, what time is it?"

Doris had quickly looked at her screen and answered automatically, "A quarter to two."

The answer had made Lotte see red.

"Doris, if you want to fit in here properly, then you have to stop talking like a 'fish head'," Lotte replied, again in broad dialect.

A 'fish head' was a derogatory term for a North German. In the eyes of South Germans like Lotte, fish was the staple diet of all those who lived close to the coast in the north of

Germany. Not that Cologne, the most celebrated city on the Rhine River, was anywhere near the coast.

Lotte tried her best to patiently explain why the South was superior to the North in every way, naturally continuing in dialect.

"In Bayreuth, here in Franconia, the clock goes round differently."

"You mean in Bavaria."

An exasperated Lotte was not going to explain that although Franconia was part of the state of Bavaria, it was only so because of a quirk of history, and that it was quite a different place entirely.

She simply replied, for the most part still in almost unintelligible dialect, "In Bavaria they say 'quarter to' just like you do. We Franconians are more intelligent. I'd never say anything as stupid as 'a quarter to'."

Doris bit back a smile.

"Lotte, you need to be more precise. What has the time of day got to do with intelligence?"

Lotte straightened herself up to make herself seem a little taller and then embarked on an exhaustive explanation.

"OK, this is how it is."

She fetched a glass and filled it with mineral water.

"So, how much is in this glass? How would you describe it?"

"Well, it's full."

"Right. And now?" Lotte took a big gulp and put the glass back on the table.

"Now? Hmmm. Three-quarters full."

"Exactly. And now?" Lotte took two gulps this time and set it down with a slight burp.

"A quarter full."

Lotte triumphantly took the last gulp and refilled the glass.

"What would you say to someone who said the glass was a quarter past empty or a quarter to full? You'd think they're not right in the head, wouldn't you? But that's exactly what you barbarians do when telling the time. A quarter past full, a quarter to full – how stupid is that! It's not 'a quarter to two', it's 'three-quarters two'. Once again, Lotte made sure to heavily emphasise her Upper Franconian pronunciation.

Right, say after me, 'three-quarters two'!"

Doris sighed. She had the uneasy feeling that she would never understand how these Upper Franconians ticked – neither how they told the time, nor how they thought, for that matter. But Lotte was right. She would have to try and learn.

"OK. Three-quarters two, then," Doris said, in her normal German accent.

Lotte grimaced, mimicking Doris.

"We're not in the Academy of Stilted Speech here. The right way is not how you said it but how I say it!"

Doris again attempted to imitate Lotte but could not get it right.

"Just imagine you've just drunk one or two little mugs of beer and then it's easier," Lotte advised, using, unfortunately, a southern German term for 'mug of beer' that Doris had never heard before.

Doris, at a loss, asked, "What am I supposed to drink?"

"Oh, for God's sake, beer! If you think you're tongue-tied, then it makes it easier – 'three-quarters two'."

Doris tried again, "Three-quarters two," this time almost getting the pronunciation right.

Lotte was partway happy, feeling she had finally got somewhere. She snatched pen and paper, scribbled something on the pad, and held it under Doris' nose.

"And this? What does this say?"

"A quarter past one."

"No, think of my glass of water."

"A quarter one?"

Fearing she had said 'quarter' in the normal German way, Doris then tried to correct herself by saying 'quarter' as close to a Franconian accent as she could.

Lotte shook her head in utter exasperation, her hair whipping around savagely.

"You'll never learn it – not 'a quarter one' but 'a quarter two'. Think of my glass of water. It's not a quarter empty if it's a quarter full."

The ringing of the telephone rescued Doris from further humiliation. Lotte answered and after only a few seconds it could be seen from the tense expression on her face that it was not about a parking offender.

"Body," she mimed across to Doris before she said aloud. "OK, we're already on our way."

By then Doris had jumped up and grabbed her denim jacket. Lotte emptied the clock glass as fast as she could and grabbed her jacket before they stormed out.

"Here we go then! We'll walk there. It'll be quicker than going to get a car."

"What's happened?"

"Female body in the Dammwäldchen. A young woman has collapsed and died; cause of death as yet unknown. Presumably a false alarm, a heart attack or something like that. But we should at least take a look."

Doris hurried after her assistant. Fortunately, she had a concrete idea of where the Dammwäldchen, a small park, lay, namely right next to RWG, Richard Wagner Grammar School. She had already gone past the Dammwäldchen on her way to the pedestrian zone and had wondered more than once how this little copse of trees had come by its name.

At most there was just a handful of trees, no more than ten lindens, set among paved paths, two or three park benches and a cement fountain, a sad affair, the water only just managing to dribble out. Directly next to the little park was a cobbled street with a massive brick building on one side that housed the Steingräber & Sons piano company. On the opposite side was the modern building of the Bayreuth branch of the Agriculture Insurance Agency, known by its German initials as SVLFG. The narrow side of the park connected to the entrance of RWG, while the side opposite led into the town centre.

All in all, the Dammwäldchen was not a particularly inviting place. If Doris had worked for the SVLFG she would not have wanted to spend her lunch breaks there. Instead, she would have gone on a bit further into the inner-city pedestrian zone, or a bit further still to the Palace Garden, both much more inviting places. Now and then, students from RWG would stray into the Dammwäldchen to smooch with a boyfriend or smoke, and in good weather, people who looked like they could not hope to expect much more out of life would sometimes lounge on the park benches.

Doris could have no inkling that the Dammwäldchen had been nothing more than a parking lot only a few decades earlier, hotly contested by the office workers of the SVLFG. They tolerated the trees out of necessity but always looked at them warily because the honeydew dropped by the aphids formed a sticky layer all over their cars. Looked at this way, the Dammwäldchen had undergone considerable improvement.

Doris secretly doubted it was now going to experience unfortunate celebrity as the scene of a major crime. In her wildest imaginings she could not conceive that this tranquil town, sunk in a deep sleep for eleven months of the year, could house a murderer. Lotte was probably right, the woman had probably suffered a heart attack, the sort of thing you were always reading about in the local paper.

Nevertheless, she sounded a note of caution.

"Lotte, don't come to any premature conclusions. We know absolutely nothing yet, so we should remain open to all possibilities."

The emergency doctor's car stood next to the ambulance in the small entrance between RWG and the SVLFG offices and was the first thing to be seen when the two investigators arrived. The little pseudo-forest had already been carefully cordoned off by police tape to hold back onlookers, but with dubious success. Curious office workers were crammed at the windows of the SVLFG, and in front of RWG there were passers-by and even some students trying to catch a glimpse of the goings-on.

Doris and Lotte ducked under the tape and had a quick look around. The young woman lay right in front of the fountain. The paramedics had already given her away and had packed up their things. One of them evidently knew Lotte, gesturing to her with a helpless shrug of the shoulders. Doris briefly asked herself at which party he had met her, but then purposefully pushed this thought to one side. Her assistant's private life was her affair and here everyone knew everybody else anyway.

"There was nothing we could do. Poor thing. So young. It's always particularly bad when they still have all their life ahead of them."

Lotte nodded sadly in agreement and pointed to Doris.

"My new boss, Detective Chief Superintendent Lech. You don't already know her, do you?"

"Hello, Frau Lech. Stefan Bärnrieder."

"Did you find any papers on the dead person?" Doris wanted to know.

Bärnrieder nodded, "Yes. Judging by the ID we're dealing with a Tina Hermann. 23 years old. From Bayreuth."

Lotte was shocked.

"Tina Hermann? Good heavens, I know her. She was in the year below me at RWG and, if I'm not wrong, her sister Anna is in the same year as my sister. That really is bad. Have you found out how she died?"

But the paramedic could not answer this question.

"You'll have to ask the emergency doctor, Dr Kollrab. He fancies himself as an amateur pathologist. He'll make sure he examines her thoroughly and won't give up until he finds something out. I have to get going. Will I see you at the beer festival?"

Lotte nodded and looked dreamily at the young man.

"Sure, if I don't have to do overtime."

Doris brought her back to reality.

"This Dr Kollrab, what is it with him? Why amateur pathologist?"

"Oh, he's always really excited when he gets called out to a body. It seems he's considered applying for pathology at Erlangen a few times, but he's a dyed-in-the-wool Bayreuth native, so he has found it hard to make the decision to uproot himself. That's why he has stayed here."

The doctor had found out that the two criminal investigators had arrived and sought them out.

Kollrab identified himself and used a South German greeting that had jarred with Doris when she first arrived, but she had been in Bayreuth long enough to no longer notice it.

"We've not yet been introduced. Up to now I've only dealt with your predecessor, Detective Chief Superintendent Lehmann," he said to Doris.

Lotte earned a friendly nod from him.

Doris introduced herself and got straight down to business. What had he already found out?

Dr Kollrab sighed and pointed at the dead person with a wistful expression on his face.

"So sad when someone so young ends up six feet under. But from a criminal investigative point of view, a very interesting case. Nothing so simple as a heart attack. Not that I can yet tell you the exact cause of death, but I consider a natural cause rather unlikely. Look here. At first it looks as if she suffered a fainting fit and went to the fountain perhaps to try and splash some water in her face to revive herself. And then? Drowned? A possibility is that she fainted, collapsed, and fell face first into the fountain, only then eventually falling to the ground. But that explanation is nonsense because why wouldn't she have fallen straight to the ground if she'd fainted. What other possibilities? Was there someone else involved? Was she drowned? That too I think is unlikely because I haven't found any sign of the use of violence, nor is her hair really wet. What's left, then? Not much, besides a puncture mark in the vicinity of her neck. And so, everything is speculation until she's examined by pathology. Was she injected with an anaesthetic that made her defenceless? And would she then have drowned without the need to use violence? Or are hard drugs in play here? An overdose, a fatal hit? In the neck? Would she inject herself there, at that spot? Highly unlikely. Therefore, it is my humble opinion that you should lead an investigation into her death. At the very least the involvement of another person can't be ruled out. How I'd love to go to pathology in Erlangen and examine the poor creature more closely myself …"

Kollrab was only reluctantly prepared to hand the corpse over to the emergency team who were organising the transfer to the pathology laboratory.

Lotte had to smile despite her dismay at the death.

"Our Dr Kollrab is always like that. He's definitely a loss to pathology. He always thinks all his Christmases have come at once when he's called out to a corpse. But it's more like hard work for us, isn't it?"

Doris saw it exactly the same way. She moved closer to the body and as usual when she saw a corpse, she gasped involuntarily. It always felt like the ice-cold hand of death was stroking her back, and every time she shivered. The young woman, who lay on the grimy ground in front of the fountain, had been very pretty. Her long blond hair was wet at the ends. She had probably slid down from the fountain and had only then dipped her hair in the water. There was a large scratch visible on her face. Doris presumed that this had come from the cement edge of the fountain.

"You poor thing, what happened to you?" Doris murmured to herself.

A young patrolman had just put the dead person's purse into a bag and looked at her completely at a loss what to do with it.

"Forensics are on the way, they'll take it."

Apparently, Bayreuth really was a quiet backwater. That would explain why they did not know the routine. She looked around with a searching gaze, trying to imprint every detail on her memory.

There was a large travel bag on a wooden bench only a few steps from the fountain. Curious, Doris went over to it and put on some gloves before she carefully opened the zip and looked inside. In it were several thin plastic bags, neatly stacked. They looked to contain freshly dry-cleaned clothing. Forensics would examine it as well.

She went back to Lotte.

"Have you found her phone?" she asked.

Lotte indicated with a shake of her head and a shrug of her shoulders that unfortunately there was no trace of it.

"No phone. That is strange."

"But we have found an odd outfit that looks like a costume from an old movie. It's a dark blue woollen skirt that looks like it was stolen from my great-great-grandmother. It lay right next to the body by the fountain. I've packed it up for forensics."

"Besides that, is there anything else I should know about?"

Lotte shook her head again and her hair flew wildly all over the place.

"But perhaps we should go over to RWG. My sister, Lisa, is rehearsing a production and as far as I know, Tina's sister, Anna, is also in the theatre group. She shouldn't hear it from a complete stranger, from one of the blabbermouths hanging around here, but from us."

"Good thinking, Lotte. Let's go."

28

Walking over to the school, Lotte asked what was in the travel bag.

"Looks like items of clothing, freshly dry-cleaned. I didn't take a closer look."

"Ah, now I remember – there's something different about the costumes for the play they're rehearsing right now. Lisa said something about it at home, that the clothes had been found in a really old chest. Maybe it has something to do with that."

Lotte energetically swung open the heavy wooden gate to the school and went on ahead. Doris followed her. The first thing she did stepping onto the school grounds was suck in a deep breath of school air that immediately reminded her of her own time at school, that familiar mixture of smells coming out of the old buildings: the aroma of paper; the hint of the scent of coloured pencils; the smell of innumerable students. It was simply unforgettable. Recollecting herself, she hurried to catch up with her assistant and rushed alongside her to the auditorium where the rehearsal was taking place.

Just as they reached it, the door was energetically swung open. The two detectives briefly heard snippets of dialogue carried on the whoosh of air before the door closed again with a dull thud. Lisa had dashed out and almost run over her big sister.

"Hey, Lotte – what are you doing here? Aren't you at work?" she asked in surprise.

"I'm here connected with work, unfortunately. This is my boss, Chief Inspector Doris Lech – my sister, Lisa."

"Do you have any idea what just happened in the Dammwäldchen? All we know is that an ambulance drove up and now Frau Grimm has sent me out to find out what's going on because nobody can concentrate properly."

Lisa looked like she would almost burst with curiosity, but she was going to be disappointed. Lotte exchanged a brief glance with Doris and saw the inaudible 'no' in her eyes. She quickly deflected her sister's enthusiasm.

"I'll tell you later, but I've got a question for you. The other day you were telling me about your play and the old clothes that have been found. What exactly were you talking about?"

"Typical of you, Lotte – don't you ever listen properly? We're doing this old play for the school anniversary and when we found the chest with the clothes, we decided to do the play in the original costumes from those days. Anna then took the whole lot to her sister, Tina, because she has a part-time job in a dry cleaner's and could get them cleaned for us at a reduced rate. According to Frau Grimm, they're made out of some weird woollen material you can't wash in a machine because it becomes matted. So, we had to get the clothes dry-cleaned somewhere. And Tina was actually going to bring them back today, but she has probably been held up."

The connection was now clear to Doris – she remembered that Lena, her landlady's daughter, had talked about the school play on the way to Emtmannsberg.

She butted in.

"Lisa, I've got a question I'd like to ask you before everything comes out. You're a friend of Anna's, aren't you?"

The girl nodded.

"Yeah, sure. But why do you want to know?"

"It's about her sister, Tina. Has Anna told you anything about her? What I mean is, more than she worked part-time at a dry cleaner's? Do you know anything else about her?"

"Oh-oh – has Tina done something wrong? I know she's studying law and is doing work experience with a lawyer at the moment. He's called Dr Held. How weird having a name meaning 'hero'. I remember the name because Anna is always making jokes about Tina's 'hero'."

"Anything else? It doesn't matter how unimportant it might seem to you; it can still be meaningful to us."

"Hell, has she really done something silly? I can't imagine her doing anything like that. She always seems so responsible and in control. And so fashionable. At least, she has been lately. She used to always run around in grey hoodies and jeans, or even tracksuit pants, but in the last few months she has totally changed what she wears. Now she often looks really supercool – high heels and designer clothes, super stylish. Anna says that she no longer shops in the mall, in the Rotmaincenter, because all the fashions there are too boring. She prefers to make the trip down the freeway to Ingolstadt Village and buy designer clothes there. They're not as expensive as in a brand-name store but they're still genuine designer labels."

Doris pricked up her ears. This really was information that could be of interest. So, she probed further.

"And have you and Anna discussed how Tina can afford all her new clothes? They would cost a fortune."

Lisa wrinkled up her nose considering this. She looked so much like her sister, Lotte, at that moment, that Doris could not help smiling.

"If she really has done something silly, I don't want to land her in it. I don't exactly know. We've just speculated. Anna thinks that Tina might have a boyfriend who is paying for it all. That's to say, a really rich sugar daddy type of boyfriend.

In the end, we decided it must be her 'hero', Dr Held. That's why we've always been making jokes about him. Apart from that, last spring Tina also had something going with some guy she wanted to take home. Oddly, she never did. It was just after that she started buying different clothes. It was in the beginning of May that she started work experience with Dr Held, doing hours here and there and then longer stints in the university holidays."

There was not any more information to get out of the girl, so Doris deliberately ended the conversation.

"Listen, Lisa – we're now going to go into the auditorium and Lotte will tell all of you what has just happened. At the same time, I'll talk to Anna and your teacher, Frau Grimm. It's important you keep your mouth shut and let your sister speak, OK?"

Lisa nodded. Her face radiated a mixture of surprise and curiosity.

"OK."

All three stepped into the auditorium, where Doris immediately turned to the teacher, Frau Grimm, and drew her to one side. She introduced herself quietly and asked her to come out of the room with Anna. Hesitantly, the girl followed them outside, where Doris introduced herself to her.

"Can we sit down somewhere, somewhere we can talk undisturbed? A staff room perhaps?"

Without saying a word Frau Grimm nodded and led them into the administration corridor where there were several staff rooms. One of them was occupied by a couple of teachers but they had luck with the second one.

In the meantime, Lotte had the thankless task of letting a horde of young girls, who for the most part she knew personally, learn the news of Tina's death. She spoke slowly and deliberately, weighing every word carefully.

"Well, you've already asked yourselves what happened in the Dammwäldchen and why the police are here. Unfortunately, I have to tell you some very sad news: Anna's big sister, Tina, has been found dead next to the fountain. How she died, well, we still don't know. But as long as the cause of death hasn't been established, it will remain a high priority investigation."

The girls all began talking excitedly at once, some going pale, others jumping up and wrapping themselves crying around each other's necks. Others still just anxiously cracked their fingers. But the news left no girl unaffected. Lotte gave them a few minutes to take it in but then raised her hand and went on.

"I'm sure that soon the first speculation will begin on social media. And I'm sure you'll all be able to follow it there, but for the moment put your phones down and listen to me again. Tina had a bag of dry-cleaned clothes with her. They were your costumes, weren't they?"

Unanimous nodding. One girl named Tanja explained, "Yes, she was going to have them dry-cleaned for us. She had a job in the Eysserhauspassage – what was the place's name again?"

"No need to remember it – we've already heard about it. Do any of you know anything else about Tina? She's supposed to have changed a lot, lately. Has Anna ever said anything about it?"

Tanja tilted her head and then nodded.

"Anna only said that her sister wanted to fly to Rome for a weekend trip and from there go to Fashion Week in Milan. She had got tickets to the Fashion Gala. Anna also said that her friends here were too dowdy and besides, none of them wanted to go with her, and that she just wanted out of this provincial backwater and that she was now going to make big money. On social media you're always seeing people who become millionaires when they're still really young. She didn't want to waste any time but wanted to become rich while she was still young enough to enjoy life."

Another girl, Julia, added, "When I was at Anna's just a few days ago this slimy gold chain type of guy arrived and picked Tina up. She was dressed to the nines and had laughed when she said hello, but it was obvious that it was really put on. Anna says that she always waits for him standing in front of the neighbour's house, a big mansion, because her own home is too plain. I only saw the two of them by accident; I was just arriving as they were both getting into the car. It was some kind of sports car but not a Porsche. A Lamborghini maybe? Could that be right? I'm not sure; I don't know much about cars. Anyway, it went with the guy. Anna said that they'd never laid eyes on him, that Tina had never introduced him. Apparently, she was scared her family wasn't good enough for such a poser."

Lotte eagerly wrote down all the girls' testimonies but besides what Tanja and Julia had told her there was nothing that they could really go on. Eventually she decided to send the students home.

"I think you can go now. The investigation is definitely finished for today so there's nothing more to keep you here. Thank you for your help. And don't take it all too personally. You couldn't have changed anything. But I have a big request of all of you – look after Anna. Simply be there for her, but, of course, without pressuring her. She needs good friends right now."

Lotte ran into her boss, who looked visibly worn out, in the corridor.

"Oh, Lotte, it was bad. Anna has completely collapsed. I'm taking her home now. Her parents have to be informed, too. Frau Grimm knows the family very well and is coming with me. That's a relief, I can tell you. In the meantime, find out if there is anything new from forensics or pathology. We'll meet up back at the station, OK?"

29

Arriving back at Blackthorn Mill, Rudolf feverishly considered where he could hide the pages of sheet music. Eventually, he decided to stash them under the kitchen stove where the wood was stored, covering them with the firewood that was waiting there to meet its fate. Meanwhile, it had become dark and soon it would be dinnertime. The wood already burning in the stove would easily last out the night. Nobody would find the music. And as soon as the children were asleep, he would tell his wife everything and next morning carry the music to the barn in the wood basket. That would be inconspicuous. Nobody would presume it was hidden there, even if he were seen, which was highly unlikely. He would hide the music under a loose board in the back corner of the barn, where the few work tools that he possessed were already stored. It would be safe there.

Rudolf was unusually restive at dinner, so much so that his wife, Anneliese, repeatedly cast him searching looks. He slid nervously around on his chair, again and again looking anxiously towards the window and in the end standing up and drawing the threadbare curtains closed.

"What on earth is wrong with you?" she wanted to know.

Rudolf fobbed his wife off, answering gruffly, "Can't you hear how the east wind is whistling? And if the curtains don't hold out much of the cold, I'm still glad for the little they do."

He could hardly wait till the table was cleared and Margarethe had finished the washing up. He breathed out loudly and sharply when his daughter sat herself down again at the table and pulled out her homework.

"What are you doing now?" he asked her, louder than he intended.

Margarethe looked up in surprise, explaining, "I'm sorry, I still have homework I have to finish."

"Can't you do it during the day? What do you do with yourself all day, anyway? Daydream?"

He knew he was being unjust, but the suspense was making him react irritably.

"Rudolf, please! She helped me with patching in the afternoon. It has to be done in daylight otherwise the work is slipshod. Let the girl do her homework. Why don't you go and help the boys? There are still some sacks of flour to be loaded."

Rudolf was more than relieved when his sons, tired from their physical work in the mill, finally went to bed. Margarethe, too, packed her school things away, wished them good night and went upstairs. He waited a quarter of an hour and then beckoned to his wife to join him on the sofa.

"Sit down, wife. I have something to tell you."

Hesitantly, Annaliese slid next to him and looked him searchingly in the eye.

"What's wrong with you? Since this afternoon you've been so different, so restless."

"I've found something that will help us through the winter, no – help us through the whole war, however long it may last."

He managed a nervous smile but could not at the same time meet her gaze. That unsettled her even more. She clearly sensed that something was coming that was not good –

something sinister, frightening. A slight shudder went through her, and she felt goosebumps all over her body. She tried hard to suppress this sense of foreboding. Of course, she did not yet know what it was going to be about. Perhaps it would be less harmful than she feared?

She forced herself to ask in a carefree tone of voice, "Really? What is it? Show me!"

Rudolf stood up and went over to the wood stack. He laboriously pulled the pages of music out from under the logs and went slowly back to the sofa, holding them out to Anneliese.

"Here."

She grabbed them and studied them uncomprehendingly. She knew nothing about music beyond being able to identify the notes, and she had only been taught that by Rudolf because he had insisted. She could neither translate what she saw into a melody, nor did she notice the dedication.

"And?" She was at a loss.

Rudolf sighed softly.

"You really don't know, do you? What it is, what it means."

Now Anneliese became indignant, hissing sharply, "If I had, I wouldn't have asked!"

Rudolf backed down. He didn't want to make her angry. It was going to be difficult enough to get her to come over to his side. He put a calming arm around her and drew her a little closer.

"Anneliese, it's like this. I found these pages of music today in the Zweistein's piano. Albert must have hidden them there. Look here, there's a dedication on them. 'For my beloved A'. It must be referring to him. I have long had the suspicion that poor Albert is, let us say, oriented differently

from other men, and that this is a thorn in the side of Zweistein senior. And do you know what? It's exactly this fact that provides me with an opportunity. If I threaten Albert with showing them to his father, he will eat out of my hand. And that means for us that we can put meat on the table every Sunday and, even better, not have to suffer any other type of deprivation either. You'll see, these pages of music are worth their weight in gold – or, still better, in ham."

Now Rudolf's smile was genuine. He would be able to do something beneficial for his family, to care for them how it was proper for a father of a family to do. He was therefore all the more surprised when he met a furious response from his wife.

"Have you gone completely mad, running off with this music? How can you be so stupid? Don't you realise you'll be the first person suspicion will fall on? They'll notice it's missing and then you'll be in for it. You'll never get another position anywhere if you've been in prison. Or, even worse, as a former prisoner, you'll be one of the very first sent to the front. How can you do something like this to your family?"

Shocked by this loud outburst, he quickly laid his index finger across Anneliese's lips.

"Annie, calm down! I'm sure the police won't be told. It's something the old man will want swept under the carpet, and the son just as much. Perhaps he's hidden the music from his father so that he doesn't find out about his unnatural love affair. For I'm certain of one thing: the dear boy loves men. Then again, he may have hidden it because he's planning to do something with the music that makes it imperative that the actual composer doesn't become known. I have no idea what that something might be. Perhaps that person doesn't want to be associated with the piece. Or perhaps the lad wants to

claim all the glory for himself. There must be some reason for the music being hidden in the piano. And as long as I have the music, I can't see why I can't take advantage of it. And the other part of the dedication, 'from S.W. In Everlasting Remembrance'. Who knows who this S.W. is? Definitely a man. And if I were to go out on a limb, then only one name occurs to me: Siegfried Wagner, the son of the opera composer. And I've had a good look at the whole piece; someone who knows what they're doing composed it. Just imagine for a moment if Siegfried and Albert … if that were to become public. I would think it's even more important for Siegfried than Albert that it doesn't become known. I mean, his wife had a son just a few weeks ago. What's his name again? Wieland? And her? Winifred, isn't it?"

Anneliese nodded mechanically. Red blotches were forming crazily on her cheeks.

"You're going to stir up a hornets' nest, Rudolf. Believe me, it will come to no good. You simply mustn't do it!"

"Come on! What can possibly go wrong? I'll make sure the music is well hidden and then, to begin with, I'll sound out Albert. If he won't do what I hope, then I'll visit Herr Wagner. And the prospect that I might visit his wife and son should be enough to turn him into the goose that lays the golden egg."

His wife began to cry. Pure horror gripped her. It wouldn't, it couldn't turn out well.

"Rudolf, I'm pleading with you, let go of this insane idea! Nothing good can come of it. We've never had anything to do with the police, nor have we ever done anything wrong. Please, let's stop here. Take the pages back to where you found them, and all will be well."

Rudolf took her tear-drenched face in his hands and forced her to look him in the eye. Imploringly he replied, "Wife, don't be silly. I can't take the music back. Take for granted that Albert would be on the alert and search me the next time I stepped onto the estate. Then I really would land straight in jail. And even if I did manage to put it back without being noticed, if he in the meantime has noticed it missing and then finds it suddenly back in the piano – then he'd know exactly who took it. That would only mean that I would lose my leverage over him and who knows what he'd do to me then. No, I simply can't take it back."

Anneliese cried even more. Everything that she still had, everything that she possessed, she was seeing lost at that very moment, slipping through her fingers because of the lunacy of her husband.

"All right, good. If you don't want or can't take it back, and there's no way I could, then we'll have to burn it so nobody can find it. And you're not going to blackmail either Albert or this Siegfried Wagner, do you hear? You have to promise me that. It has to be as if you never found this music. Promise me that!"

Rudolf's only response was an ill-tempered growl, which in no way placated his wife. She only became louder, and her tone of voice swung from fear to displeasure.

"Rudolf, can't you hear me? You mustn't turn into a criminal. How will we be able to look you in the eye again? I beg you, burn the music. Or, if you can't, give the sheets to me and I'll throw them in the stove."

He looked askance in annoyance, rolled the pages of music together and stuffed them into the sleeve of his shirt, which ballooned out, thick and misshapen.

"All right then, wife! If you'd rather go hungry, then I'll destroy them. But I'll do it! Do you hear, I'll do it! And not here in the stove but outside in the forest. We don't want unholy ashes to contaminate us in the house, do we? Are you content, now? First thing tomorrow morning I'll set fire to them outside and bury the ashes in the wood."

Anneliese remained sceptical. Again, he couldn't return her searching gaze and that made her worry that he would lie just to appease her.

Wracked by anxiety, she begged him, "Rudolf, do you honestly mean that? Please, I don't want to lose you because of such stupidity. You're still planning on blackmail; I can see it in you. It will not go well. Please, you have to promise me – this music is going to be a disaster for the whole family. If you still have a spark of love for me then destroy it. I'm imploring you, do it! If not for me, then for our children. It's simply not worth it, believe me."

Finally, Rudolf answered begrudgingly, "For heaven's sake, if you want it so much then I'll do it. I can't understand you – it would be the opportunity for us to finally get a piece of the cake. And you want to give up this chance just because you're afraid of something that won't happen. But all right, I'll do it. Only don't complain to me anymore that we don't have enough money."

Abruptly, he stood up and left the kitchen. His wife sat there crying. She flinched when the kitchen door slammed. She strained to hear the receding footsteps and then just made out the front door being slammed as well. She would have loved to spring up and rush to the window to see where her husband had gone, but it was dark outside, and she would not be able to see anything. He, on the other hand, would see her clearly at the lighted window and know that she did not trust him. That would make everything even worse. So, she stayed sitting for what felt like an eternity, waiting for his footsteps to return.

Rudolf strode out into the cold without putting anything warm on. He was furious: at his wife for making what he had done weigh on his conscience even more than it had up to then; and at himself, for having let himself be carried away by something so idiotic.

It was clear to him that there was no going back, but it would be madness to actually destroy the music. Holding on to it protected him and those he loved more than it placed them in harm's way. Breathing heavily, he went over to the barn and turned, staring searchingly into the darkness, as if it were possible to see if someone was watching him. He was thinking less about Anneliese than about Albert, who might already have discovered his loss and put two and two together. He had to be careful.

The frost had sharpened under the clear, star-filled sky, but Rudolf barely felt its bite. Quickly and silently, he went into the barn, prised a board from the floor and lay the pages down in the cavity. As long as the temperature stayed below freezing the sheets would be secure without protective wrapping, but he would return in the next few days with a tin can to put the sheets in and a cloth soaked in oil to wrap around the can. He then carefully arranged everything as it had been before, spread straw in the corner and walked back to the house. He did not return to the kitchen because he felt even less able to look his wife in the eye than he did before. Instead, the old staircase creaked as he went up to the bedroom, where he immediately lay down in bed and pretended to sleep.

Anneliese, who obviously heard him return, still waited a few minutes before following him upstairs. She did not have to talk to him again because he had closed his eyes and was taking deep and regular breaths. She was not stupid. She knew he had not done anything, had not burned the music, but had certainly hidden it. It would not do any good to beg him again.

She was convinced evil would take its own course.

30

The visit to the Hermann family was anything but pleasant. Anna, completely beside herself, fell sobbing round her mother's neck as soon as the front door opened. Before Doris could say anything, the girl had already blurted out, "Mum, Tina is dead! They found her in the Dammwäldchen."

Frau Hermann swayed and went ashen.

"No, it's not true," she whispered tonelessly. Doris did not answer – what was there to say? But when the shocked woman looked the chief inspector and the teacher in the eye, she knew it was true.

"It's not true. It's not true," she now cried out audibly and Frau Grimm took her gently by the arm and led her into the house.

She eased her into an armchair in the living room and ran to the kitchen to fetch her something to drink.

Attracted by the screaming, Herr Hermann came in too. He had been in the cellar.

"What's going on here? And who are you?" he asked gruffly, standing at the open door. He crossed the room with quick strides and put his arm round his wife, sitting there paralysed.

"Detective Chief Superintendent Doris Lech. Herr Hermann, I have to give you some tragic news. Your daughter, Tina, was found dead about an hour ago in the Dammwäldchen. We can't exclude murder, and so we've begun an investigation."

The man stared at her uncomprehendingly. His expression revealed he was finding it difficult to process this terrible news.

"Murder? Are you mad? Who would want to murder our Tina? She hasn't done anything to anyone. Or has some bastard tried ..."

Doris understood without it being spelled out and was immeasurably relieved to at least be able to rule out this presumption.

"No, we can just about exclude that possibility. Naturally we have to wait for the pathology report, but at the moment there is nothing that points to anyone having indecently assaulted your daughter. Perhaps you could help us with the progress of our investigation and tell us a bit about Tina? Who did she go to meet, what were her habits, where did she usually go out to, who were her close circle of friends? Things like that. But also striking changes in her behaviour recently. Everything like that could help us."

"I've seen this coming for ages, I've had such fears about Tina, but she didn't want to talk to me," her mother sobbed.

Throughout this exchange, Anna had just sat on the sofa without joining in, too shocked for any more tears. Even when Frau Grimm returned with a bottle of mineral water and a few glasses, the girl didn't react. Instead, Frau Grimm sat down close to her on the sofa and began stroking her hair consolingly. Anna cuddled up to her teacher, seeking something to cling to, without really being aware of her presence. She had slipped completely into another world and no more information would be got out of her while she was so lost in her own thoughts.

So Doris concentrated on Frau Hermann.

"What do you mean by 'seeing this coming'?" she wanted to know. "Did Tina ever drop any hints? Did you notice anything different? Did anything strike you in particular?"

The mother swallowed, brought herself under control and loudly blew her nose.

"She didn't drop any hints. Only, this spring she was so changed all of a sudden. So happy, freshly in love, on cloud nine. She wanted to introduce us to her new man, but nothing ever came of it. On the day that he was invited to dinner there was apparently an argument between the two of them and that was the end of that."

"From then on, she became totally closed as far as we were concerned. She changed her whole image. Before, she was someone who didn't care much about outward appearances; she was most comfortable in a sweatshirt and jeans, or at home, in tracksuit pants – the most important thing for her was that her clothes were comfortable. But as soon as she finished with this man, she was all of a sudden not the old Tina anymore: brand-name clothes, high heels, stylish, and heavily made up. I suddenly had the feeling that we were no longer good enough for her. She never told us who she went out with, or where. Apparently, she now and then went to exotic places, to Italy, or sometimes to Berlin or Munich. I asked her again and again where the money was coming from for these trips, but she only laughed at me and said that that was the least of her problems."

"But sometimes she was completely different. Those times, if she was staying home for the evening, she would cuddle up to me on the sofa just like Anna is doing now with Frau Grimm. But you couldn't talk to her at those times. If you tried, she would immediately close up again. I'm sure she had secrets she didn't tell us, and not good ones, either."

Doris nodded thoughtfully. She had already guessed something similar. What counted now was to find proof for these suspicions.

"Frau Hermann, I'm sure your daughter would have had a mobile phone. Is it possible that she left it home by mistake?"

"I can't imagine her doing that but I'm happy to try and look for it. I'll just be a moment."

She went up the stairs, her phone in her hand, and rang her dead daughter's phone. After less than a minute she was back in the living room.

"No, it doesn't seem to be here, although she may have put it on silent. But she never did that. Has it disappeared? That's very strange?"

The chief inspector thought so, too. These days you couldn't run into any young person without a mobile phone. Perhaps someone took it off her to destroy evidence?

"Listen, I would like very much to take Tina's computer with me and give it over to forensics. Perhaps they'll be able to find something on it that will help with the investigation. She does have a computer, doesn't she? And I would also like to take a look at Tina's room, even if it is difficult for you at the moment."

Frau Hermann motioned her to come with her. Without saying a word, she went ahead across the hall and silently opened a door. Doris found herself in a modern and austere room, surrounded by white furniture and prints that lacked a common theme, prints she thought would take some time to get used to.

"Did Tina keep anything like a diary?" she asked, although she could hardly imagine she had. Who still kept a diary these days?

"Frau … Lech, that was your name, wasn't it? Do you really think I would have known that? I didn't spy on her, and she never mentioned anything like that. But take your time looking around – perhaps you'll be lucky."

Tina's mother disappeared and Doris found herself standing alone in the room. One of the windows was partially open and the sound of children's laughter could be heard from outside. Just a few years ago it would have been Tina playing and laughing in the park – and now she was dead. The still childless chief inspector felt a tinge of sadness. The thought struck her that at least she would be spared a loss like this.

She set about carefully searching through cupboards, the desk, and the night table. In the desk drawer she discovered a thin exercise book and when she opened it, she was surprised to find Tina had written poems in it. She flew over the verses – they were, without exception, love poems, and they all seemed to be expressing longing and sadness. She couldn't find any indication revealing when Tina had written them, but she had obviously been very unhappy in that phase of her life.

Doris put the exercise book back and opened the cupboard doors. She was confronted by expensive designer clothes worth several thousand euros lined up next to each other. With a shake of her head, she closed the doors again. Where the heck had the girl got the money from? Quite obviously, Tina Hermann had lived a double life, otherwise there was no explanation for all these expensive things. However, as there were no obvious clues, Doris clamped the notebook computer under her arm and said her goodbyes to the mourning family.

Frau Grimm silently let her know that she would stay on.

31

Albert waited patiently for his father to leave the house. His mother had gone into Bayreuth, taking Lisette with her to be dropped off at the 'broomstick stable'. Seeming to take forever, Zweistein senior finally finished tying the laces of his sturdy winter boots and putting on his winter jacket.

He nodded to his son and growled, more to himself than to his son, "Well, I better be off. I'll be away at least until Monday," and, without waiting for a response, trudged out into the icy cold.

Albert still waited till the coach had rolled out of the courtyard before running into the drawing room and almost reverently opening the piano. Now at long last he would be able to play the piece that Siegfried had written expressly for him. His anticipation made him shudder. It was almost as if Siegfried was in the room with him, as if he were about to put his arm around him and stroke him affectionately. It was far too seldom that the two men were able to meet. At any rate, it had become more complicated, even though Siegfried's wife, Winifred, was hardly any problem at all, being more than busy with the new-born. Zweistein senior was the problem. It was he they feared the most. He watched them like a gun dog. There would be a scandal and a half if he were ever to catch them.

Albert reached inside the piano to fetch out the sheet music, but his fingers could not feel any paper. He reached further, stretching his fingers out as far as he could, but found nothing. Frantically, he removed the front board of the piano, only held in place by wooden pins. But even then, with the hammers and strings in full view, he could not find the music.

The young man was gripped by panic. Could his father in fact have found the handwritten sheets of music? His heart missed a beat. That would be the last straw. Albert was convinced that if he found the music his father would disinherit him. He wanted to put the piano back together again, but he was so jumpy and clumsy that the front board slipped out of his grasp and crashed with a loud bang on the floor. A fine split was visible in the veneer and Albert felt for a moment that he would faint. Then he took a deep breath that calmed him down a little. He shooed a maidservant, who had been attracted by the noise, back into the kitchen, explaining that he was just wanting to study the mechanics of the instrument. Then he put the front board back, this time more carefully. The small bit of damage was hardly noticeable and so he hoped his parents would not notice it. He played a few quick passages, some loudly and some softly – and could not hear anything different. Relieved, he closed the lid over the keys and tried to order his thoughts.

If his father had actually found the music. then a storm of unparalleled proportions would already have broken over his head. His father was a very impulsive man who would not have kept his feelings concealed. But who else could have taken the music? He next settled on his sister. Lisette had to practise daily, even if she did so begrudgingly and got out of it whenever she could. It was quite conceivable that out of boredom she might have looked into the piano to see how it worked. On the other hand – no! It was exactly for that reason that Albert had hidden the music in the piano in the first place. He was absolutely sure Lisette had no interest in the inner workings of the instrument she so hated. So, it could not have been her. Who was there left? As much as Albert wracked his brains, he could think of no one. Not even Schlehmüller could have pilfered them because he was never alone in the drawing room, always being there together with his student. And why would the piano teacher open the instrument? No, that made no sense. So, it must have been Lisette.

He would present Old Willi with a day off and instead pick her up from school himself. That would provide him with the opportunity to drill deeper into what his sister knew about the affair.

32

Chief Inspector Doris Lech and her assistant were leaning, heads together, over the laptop opened up on her desk. Tabea Schmidt from the Forensic Investigation Branch, generally referred to by its German acronym, KTU, was standing next to them with a satisfied smile on her face. She had worked fast. Doris acknowledged the fact with a nod.

"Well done, Tabea. You've made fantastic progress. Congratulations."

Tabea blushed and tried to downplay the praise.

"Thanks for the accolades but it was really easy. You could've done it yourself. The password was plain and simple, 'TinaAnna'. We got in straight away. Apart from first and last names, and birthdays, a combination of names is the next most likely possibility for a password. If that hadn't worked, we would have run algorithms that do the job. They just take a bit longer because they've got to go through every possibility."

"I also let myself do a little poking around. The victim had photographed several documents and put them in folders, neatly sorted. Besides that, she had made extensive searches on the internet and put the results in folders, too. For example, there's a folder called 'Eierberg Beauty Clinic' that contains an ancient newspaper article from the 1950s, and another folder called 'Crystal Spa' that contains a whole lot of photographed documents. There are also folders I haven't looked at yet, like this one called 'Weigelt', or this one,

'Business Trips'. What sort of business trips does a law student make, I'd like to know. Indulge yourselves, you've got the computer."

"Thanks, Tabea. Did you find out anything else?"

"On the computer? No, but if you want, we can look for deleted data later. Look, if I'm no longer needed here, I need to go. We've got more than enough to do in the KTU."

Doris nodded distractedly and Tabea rushed off.

"Lotte, if I only knew what we're looking for. The girl has been dead for almost a day, and we've got nothing concrete to go on. And we still haven't got the autopsy results. We're feeling around in the dark."

Lotte sighed.

"It really sucks that we're so stuck. But do you know what? Tonight, we should go and do something to take our minds off it. There's a beer festival in Bocksrück and absolutely everyone will be there. What do you say? Should we go? We're certain to bump into some people from Tina's graduation year at school. With a bit of luck, we'll find out a bit more about her, about her circle of friends, the sort of people she hung out with."

It was obvious that Lotte was searching around for a good excuse but Doris, after a brief hesitation, agreed to come along, feeling that they were getting nowhere hanging about at the police station.

"At least it's better than twiddling our thumbs and, after all, we can't keep going all night. But I've got one condition; if in the meantime we get a hot lead, then it has priority."

"Of course, boss. That goes without saying," declared Lotte as sincerely as she could.

When her phone rang, Lotte, now with a spring in her step, sprinted over to answer it. Doris had to smile. Her assistant was pretty good. What was she always saying? 'It's fine' but mangled so badly by her Franconian accent that at first she had not understood what she was saying. It applied to Lotte herself. She was 'fine' in the Franconian sense. As Doris had found out as time went on, coming out of the mouth of Franconians, people not known for their effusiveness, saying something was 'fine' was the highest praise. Doris was torn away from these thoughts about the strange new world she had landed herself in by excited waving. Lotte was trying to get the person on the other end to be patient.

"Wait a moment, I'll ask what would be the best thing to do – Doris, it's Frau Hermann. A young guy's turned up who's interested in the laptop. Do you want to take over?"

When Doris nodded, she held the handset out to her.

"It's Frau Lech here – Frau Hermann, could you describe the man for us? Did he give a name? What? Kevin Klein? And what did he look like? Like a bird of paradise? Anything more specific? Dyed-blond hair, a pompadour hairstyle like Elvis, made up did you say, and remarkably fashionably dressed. Yes, that certainly is something we can go on, thanks very much. And what exactly did he want from you?"

Frau Hermann was so excited at the other end of the line that Lotte could have listened in even if Doris had not switched on the speaker.

"He rang the doorbell and said that he was so sorry, he had just heard that Tina had died. He said he was sorry to bother me, but she had promised to send him some photos. Would it be all right for him to access her laptop so he could copy them? I told him that it wasn't convenient right now, that it wasn't the right time, but he said the photos were very important to him. I then asked him what sort of photos they were? He said that he would know them when he saw them. I said that I didn't know the password and that Anna was at school. He said, just like that, that he knew Tina well and because of that, she had told him the password. I managed to get rid of him, but he wants to come back tomorrow morning. Chief Inspector, what should I tell him then?"

Doris and Lotte exchanged looks of astonishment.

"Frau Hermann, it would be best if we could look through Tina's photos together, to see if we can find the man. And then I could give you a memory stick with the photos on it, which you could stall him with, in case he shows up again. Perhaps it is all quite harmless but perhaps it's something else again. Would it be too much trouble for you to come to the station?"

Tina's mother knocked on the door half an hour later and Doris sat down with her at the computer to scrutinise the photos, but she shook her head again and again.

"No, he's not there," she finally mumbled. Doris nodded at her encouragingly.

"It's not too terrible, Frau Hermann. My colleague will construct an identikit picture with your help so that we know, if in doubt, who we should be looking out for. And I've pre-pared a memory stick of pictures in case the guy reappears."

Tina's mother went into another room and Doris heaved a deep and frustrated sigh.

"Kevin Klein – why can't I believe that's his real name?" she groaned, annoyed.

Lotte was not used to ironic humour and promptly stepped right in it.

"Isn't that the name of an actor? And a designer?"

She earned a roll of the eyes from her boss.

"Lotte, the designer is called Calvin, not Kevin. And you wonder why I doubt it's his real name? But I have come across more improbable things in my life, so find out from the Resident's Registration Office if there is a Kevin Klein registered here. I would eat my raincoat along with its hood if you succeed."

Naturally Doris was spared having to eat such a high-fibre meal, and after languishing through the rest of the day without tangible results, they arranged to meet up in the parking lot of the beer festival. Lotte had categorically refused the suggestion to ride share.

"Look, boss, I really appreciate the thought – but who knows what might happen at the festival? Perhaps one of us will want to stay a lot longer than the other, might meet a cool guy …"

Doris stopped her short at this point because the way Lotte pronounced 'cool' in dialect was so strange that Doris wasn't sure what she had heard.

"A what?"

"A cool guy," repeated Lotte patiently.

"Oh, a cool guy!" said Doris, finally realising that the offending word was just a mangled version of 'cool'.

Nothing in Cologne had prepared her for the local dialect. As with the odd pronunciation and subtleties of meaning of the Franconian version of 'it's fine', she was gradually getting to understand it, but despite that, as now, difficulties in understanding were still coming up from time to time.

Even though they took separate cars, Doris still had to drive to the beer festival behind her assistant because otherwise, despite all the handwritten road signs showing the way, she would never have got there by herself. When she arrived, she looked around astonished.

"Wow, it really is a cool place – a party marquee and real grottos. Impressive."

Lotte laughed cheerfully. Her eyes were sparkling with adventure and her anticipation for the evening was clear to see.

"They are rock cellars. There are a few around Bayreuth. There are some in Ringsdorf at a pub called the *Stillen Zecher*."

"Where?"

"In Ringsdorf."

Doris had not heard the name before and tried to look the place up without success.

"Lotte, how do you spell it?"

"R-Ö-D-E-N-S with 'dorf' on the end."

How could 'Rödens' be pronounced 'Rings'? But Lotte didn't notice her boss shake her head in exasperation because she was already busy attracting the attention of a waitress. Doris flinched when a huge mug of beer was plonked on the table in front of her.

"That's got to be for the two of us, doesn't it?" she asked, trying to reassure herself that she didn't have to drink all of it. Lotte only laughed, snapped up her own drink and clinked mugs with her boss.

"Lotte, we still have to drive."

"Come on, boss! The night has just begun. And after this we'll just drink lemonade and cola, okay?"

Sighing, Doris nodded and drank a sip.

"Hmmm, tastes good," she discovered, and Lotte had to laugh.

"Do you think we don't know how to brew beer? Here in Upper Franconia? The place with the highest proportion of breweries per square kilometre in the country?"

Before Doris could respond, two men came over to their table and asked her and Lotte to dance. After a rushed gulp of her beer, Lotte stood up, but Doris, by contrast, took her time. For a start, she did not really like dancing. Secondly, the guy was not really her type – far too young for her taste. And thirdly, after the fiasco with her ex-boyfriend, Peter, she had had her fill of men. Consequently, she only responded in monosyllables when going up to the dance floor and not surprisingly managed to end up back at the beer table after only one dance.

Lotte, on the other hand, was having a dazzlingly good time with her dancer. The guy was certainly a sight for sore eyes, something even Doris had to unwillingly admit to herself as she observed the two of them. Despite the loud music they looked to be immersed in a lively conversation.

"Tell me, how is it possible that I've never noticed you before? Where in Bayreuth do you hang out? At Liebesbier? Ponte? Dubliner?" the charming dancer was asking her. Laughing, Lotte shook her head, so that her hair whipped wildly in all directions.

"No, I'm more someone who goes to local festivals."

"So that's the reason. I can guarantee you that if I'd already seen you around, I'd have made sure I'd found an opportunity to speak to you. You don't even need to change the way you dress, you're so stunning. Have you ever played with the idea of going into the fashion industry? As a model? It's really exciting. My friend and I, we're always looking for interesting new faces. He's a designer, you know?"

Lotte declined the offer.

"Look, you know, my job is exciting too. I don't have to go on a runway and break my legs in the stiletto heels those poor things have to wear. I can go to work in running shoes."

"And what is your exciting job?" the dancer wanted to know.

"Me? I'm with the Criminal Investigation Department."

"Wow! What, you deal with murder and manslaughter? Violent crimes and that sort of thing?" he asked, visibly interested.

Lotte was not really comfortable saying much about her job and so she quickly played down the topic.

"Yeah, let's talk about something else."

"No, no! I think it's totally exciting. I'd really like to hear more about it. Only, I just have to go see my business partner. I'll be back in two minutes, and then I'll smuggle you into the bar where you can tell me a few exciting anecdotes. I'll only be gone a moment, okay? Don't run away, princess!"

"I'd rather you told me the exciting things you do. Are you also in the fashion business?"

"In a minute. I really have to go over there straight away. I'll hurry, promise. Don't let anyone else ask you to dance – otherwise I'll be jealous!"

Lotte laughed, half amused, half genuinely flattered. She was even escorted back to her table but then her unknown dancer disappeared into the throng.

"Oh, Doris – did you see the hot guy I was with? I only hope he keeps his word and comes back. I'd sure like to dance with him again, and more besides …"

When Doris noticed the dreamy expression on Lotte's face she didn't enquire further. A clear case of love at first sight. The evening together was more or less gone. If the guy came back, Lotte would be off with him. If he did not come back, she would presumably get drunk in frustration or at least spend the rest of the night moaning.

It really was just a few minutes before he came back to their table. Doris had to admit to herself that close up he looked even better. Luckily, he wasn't her type. She rather preferred Latin looks. But she had to recognise without the least envy that Lotte had caught herself a real heartthrob.

As soon as Lotte returned to the dance floor, Doris noticed there were a few students from RWG, Richard Wagner Grammar School, Tina's old school, sitting at the next table, among them Lotte's sister, Lisa, and Tanja and Julia from the theatre group. She said hello across the table and when the girls saw her sitting alone, they motioned her to come over. They happily slid along the bench to give her space to sit.

Doris started the conversation.

"Hi girls, I wouldn't have expected to see you here. Don't you have school tomorrow?"

The schoolgirls giggled.

"So, Frau Lech – you don't have any kids of your own, do you?"

She shook her head.

"That at least explains why you asked the question. Sure, we do have school tomorrow and, yes, we're in our final year. But yes, we'll manage. And besides, we're not the only ones who'll need to be clear-headed in the morning," Tanja chuckled, with a glance in the direction of Lotte.

"Yes, do you actually know anyone here?" Doris wanted to know.

Again, the girls giggled.

"Of course we do, and if we didn't, you can get to know them quickly enough."

"Ah, I see. So, the guy that Lotte is dancing with – do all of you know him too?"

"That old fogy? No, not our type, far too old. We do know he's from Bayreuth, though, and that his funny friend is too. They're guys who think they are super cool. I don't know if they really are or not. I don't even know what they do exactly, or what their names are. You only see them now and again in Liebesbier or, in summer, at Oskar's in the Marktplatz. Maybe they're the type of guys who want to be seen. But come to think of it, I think Tina knew them. If I remember rightly, I saw her with them in town."

"Interesting. Thanks, Tanja. That's a help with the investigation. Look, you all have a great evening."

With these words Doris stood up, but the girls protested vociferously.

"Waiiit! You haven't finished your beer. You can't just simply vanish."

"Oh yes I can. I have to drive after this and besides, I really do have to be clear-headed in the morning. Good night, everyone."

Taken aback, they stared as Doris left and Lisa, quick as a flash, grabbed the half-full mug of beer for herself.

When Doris made her way down the sunken pathway to the carpark, she could hear voices behind her. Naturally, she realised that she would not be the only one going back to their car from that sort of popular festival. And, naturally, thanks to her training in the police, she knew well enough how to defend herself. Nevertheless, she felt uneasy knowing that there were at least two men behind her who she could not see. The cool fresh breeze blew snippets of conversation her way.

"The short one is totally cute, I really like her – no, I'm going to keep her for myself, we're quits – what's that supposed to mean, 'I've had my fun'? You earned the cash, not me."

"We've both had our fun – yes, it went pear-shaped – come on, now, don't be like that."

The conversation became softer, and Doris could not understand any more. For that matter, she did not really want to hear any more. These sorts of typical macho conversations got on her nerves. However, she was not able to avoid hearing some more snippets when the wind blew more favourably in her direction.

"Should we get a few drops of our love beer out of the car. We could see how she likes it."

"So, finally you're being sensible."

"No, this time we play by my rules."

"If only she hadn't gone meddling – building sites – women are so tiresome."

By now Doris had arrived at her car and hurried to lock herself in. She slid quickly into the driver's seat and clicked the central locking. Relieved, she breathed deeply, pressed herself deep into the upholstery and observed the sunken pathway that led to the carpark.

It was not long before two men stepped out of the darkness into the carpark, lit by a full moon. The chief inspector's eyes widened involuntarily when she recognised one of the men as Lotte's dance partner. She did not let him out of her sight as he walked up to a Porsche and seemed to take something out that he hid in his jacket pocket. The two men then sauntered back to the sunken pathway and into the shadows.

Doris unlocked her phone with flying fingers and tried to ring Lotte. In vain. Perhaps she could not hear anything with all the noise. Irritated, she instead sent a text telling her to keep an eye on her admirer. Hopefully, Lotte would read it and act accordingly. For a brief moment Doris hesitated and wondered if the two of them had been talking about Lotte and whether Lotte was possibly in danger, but then she forcefully pushed these thoughts aside. As shady as these two guys sounded, they had several other possible targets. And Lotte could look after herself, Doris was sure of that.

33

Albert endured a restless morning. He lunched just with his mother, his father still being away. His thoughts fluttered around chaotically, and he despairingly asked himself again and again what on earth could have happened to the sheet music. What if his quite personal tragedy was about to take its inevitable course. Small wonder that he only spoke in monosyllables and that his mother became increasingly suspicious.

She eventually asked straight out, "Albert, what's wrong with you today? I haven't seen you so nervous in a long time. What is it? Bad news about one of your school friends at the front?"

He nodded distractedly.

"Yes, yes, that's exactly it."

The gaunt woman went pale.

"Who then? And what's happened?" she wanted to know.

But her son had not heard her. Only when she repeated herself did he stumble around for an answer, get muddled and suddenly stand up with a jolt.

"Mother, just leave me in peace. Can't you see I'm not up to a conversation today?"

So saying, he marched out of the dining room, his mother staring after him in consternation. He slipped into his warm clothes and hurried out to the stable, where he had the sleigh harnessed.

Albert arrived at the school too early and crouched freezing on the sleigh. He would have preferred to make a detour via Siegfried's, but he was clever enough to restrain himself. Anyway, Siegfried would not have been able to help him in his current predicament and it would not achieve anything to alarm his lover just yet, particularly as he still had no idea what had actually happened. The young man shoved his hands under his armpits to warm them a bit. Not even his expensive leather gloves could help him today – it had been and still was a fiercely cold February. What a hare-brained idea, to pick Lisette up himself! If only he had sent Willi, so the old coachman's fingers and toes froze instead. As if a damn half hour mattered.

Finally, the school bell rang and Albert, on tenterhooks, kept an eye out for his younger sister. She came running through the great wooden gate and his face froze even more when he saw that she was not alone, that the unspeakable Schlehmüller daughter was running alongside her. He had not even considered that this peasant's brat would be there too. It really should have been Old Willi picking them up.

Indignantly, he barked at Margarethe, "Can't you walk home for once? You're always too much trouble!"

She looked up shocked and her eyes filled with tears. For a second it crossed his mind, without the slightest sexual attraction, that the little one had become undoubtedly pretty in the last year, but this consideration did not lessen his anger in any way.

Lisette gave her brother a furious look.

"Albert, what are you on about? Father has said that Margarethe can get a lift with us whenever she likes. So, behave like a gentleman. Should she freeze on the long walk back to Blackthorn Mill?"

She turned to Margarethe.

"Come on, get on. It would be a fine state of affairs if my brother started dictating what we should or should not do over the head of my father."

Having finished rebuking Albert, she climbed up next to him on the sleigh box, where warm blankets were already laid out. She waved to her schoolfriend to climb up on the box as well and not sit herself on the spare seat at the back like usual.

Margarethe shyly climbed up after her. She did not dare look at Albert. Embarrassed, she wiped away the tears that, due to the cold, felt like pinpricks on her cheeks. Without hesitation, Lisette laid a blanket over Margarethe's legs, but it was clear to all of them that she did not do it out of friendship but only to show her brother the limits of his authority.

Albert let the horse start off without warning so that Margarethe swayed dangerously, but Lisette grabbed her arm and prevented anything harmful happening. She noticed that Margarethe was beginning to shiver. Whether it was because of the cold or fright was not clear, but she wrapped her up in the blanket with a show of care, cast another furious glance at her brother and for the rest of the trip stared out at the snow-covered landscape.

Margarethe would have preferred to start crying again and, besides, would have rather jumped from the sleigh and walked home. Only common sense prevented her. Soon it would be dark and even colder. Her toes could get frostbite in the thin boots that she was wearing. No, she had to bear the humiliation and travel with the Zweisteins.

Albert gave himself up again to his gloomy thoughts and presumptions. That his sister had snubbed him like that could only mean that it was her who had found and taken the sheet music. But what did she want to achieve? Did she think she could have him in the palm of her hand? Whatever her motives, he took good care not to say anything that could make her angry. The risk was too great that she could give something away in front of this peasant idiot that was not meant for the ears of strangers.

Contrary to normal, he did not stop when he got to the turnoff to Blackthorn Mill but steered the horse down the mill path. He noticed that both girls looked up in surprise, but he did not react to either of them by gesture or word. He drove on to Blackthorn Mill in silence, and in silence let Margarethe climb down. Her brother, Klaus, was standing at the open door to the stable and stared in astonishment at the future lord of the manor. Expressionless, Albert curtly nodded to him and turned the sleigh for home. He did not even register that Schlehmüller himself was there looking over at him with a face as pale as chalk.

He clicked his tongue and let the horse trot on.

34

Next morning, Lotte looked anything but well-rested when she arrived somewhat late at the station. Doris stifled a grin. It did not matter how well they had got on in the last few weeks, she was and always would remain Lotte's superior, and as such could not ignore the condition she was in. So she made an effort to assume a serious expression and not to speak too loudly.

"Good morning, Lotte. Well, did you keep on drinking last night?"

Her colleague grimaced.

"I could ask you back why you left so early."

"Well, I had the feeling that you were preoccupied. And besides, I knew I had to be fresh and fit for work today."

"Me too – I'm as fresh as a daisy. At least, I will be as soon as I've had some of this coffee!"

Lotte gingerly crept over to the coffee machine and poured herself a large mug of coffee.

"Aspirin?" Doris asked mockingly, but the look on Lotte's face was one of gratitude.

"Ah, yes, that wouldn't be a bad idea at all. Every part of me hurts. I haven't had such sore muscles for a long time."

Doris raised her eyebrows.

"Will I want to know why?"

"Ah, nothing dramatic. Firstly, I overdid it with the dancing. I'm a bit out of practice. And secondly, five us drove back to Emtmannsberg at two in the morning. I didn't want to drive home myself. Anyway, since my car is still at the beer festival, this morning I had to ride to work on my bike. It wasn't much fun, I can tell you."

Doris had to laugh despite herself. Lotte deserved being made fun of after overdoing it the night before.

"And let me guess. You didn't read my text about keeping an eye on your hot guy, the guy who dragged you away? I'm convinced there's something not right about him. When I was going back to my car yesterday he was there in the carpark with some other guy, and by what they were saying they wanted to spike some girl's drink. He took something out of his car and quickly hid it in his jacket pocket."

Lotte stared at her.

"Bertie? No, I don't believe it. He's such a sweetie, so nice and attentive. An old-school gentleman. He insisted I have a Prosecco and even went to the bar to get it. He said I should just stay seated and have a short break after all the dancing. He would have already ..."

She fell silent in the middle of the sentence.

"Already got it and spiked it on the way? Was that what you were just about to say?" Doris asked. "Did you drink it, Lotte?"

"No, I don't drink Prosecco. I had already told him that. But he wouldn't give up on the idea, and when I stayed with my beer he was offended. He then vanished somewhere with his buddy. That was a bit sad."

"And you really didn't drink the Prosecco?"

"No. It stayed on the table right to the end. Why should he spike my drink? That would have been pretty foolish. He knows that I'm with the police."

"You told him that?"

Lotte screwed up her nose. "Yes, right at the beginning. No, he's not that stupid. I simply don't believe it. Besides, I don't think he would be capable of doing something like that."

"Yeah, yeah – everybody knows love makes you blind," Doris murmured.

"What's that supposed to mean? I don't even know his last name and we didn't exchange phone numbers. Unfortunately …"

Lotte looked genuinely down in the dumps. This Bertie had obviously made a big impression on her. Doris decided to put an end to the discussion.

"Well, I only hope that today's enquiry doesn't confine itself to 'Bertie', but actually has to do with the murder."

"Hmmm, hmmm – but I could still … well at lunchtime … only then?"

The chief inspector slammed her hand down on the table so hard that Lotte winced and a startled pigeon flew off from the windowsill.

"Damn it, Lotte. We've got a murder to solve. That's a lot more important than lunchtime breaks and love affairs. You can stalk your Bertie when we've caught the murderer. Not before, do you understand?"

Lotte was spared a further dressing down by the arrival of Tabea from the Forensic Investigation Branch.

"Good morning. I've got something that might interest you, Frau Lech."

Doris sighed in relief.

"You found a mobile phone in Tina's clothes?"

"No, unfortunately not. No phone, and very little worthwhile, for that matter … but … there was a small piece of a brown envelope stuck on the inside of her hoodie, perhaps the glue strip got wet and a piece of the flap stuck to the material. And not only that – a tiny scrap of paper was also hanging off it. But here's the bombshell. The paper is ancient, estimated at about a hundred years old. Unfortunately, we can't find out anything else, there was nothing important written on it except for a few squiggles. But we'd hazard a guess that the paper is the same age as the clothes."

As interesting as this finding was, it didn't fit into anything.

"Yes, it's obvious that there is a connection. I just can't see what it is. As long as we don't know anything more precise about this old paper, it doesn't really help us get any further. Nevertheless, thanks for the intel," Doris murmured, more to herself than to Tabea.

Tabea went on in any case.

"The scene of the crime hasn't revealed much, unfortunately, hardly any worthwhile leads, and besides that, it was packed up far too early. But … we've found something quite different. Maybe you can get somewhere with this."

She waved a memory stick around and let it fall into Lotte's outstretched hand. She put Tina's computer on the desk.

"Krause from our IT-team had another look at the computer and as if by magic retrieved a bunch of deleted files. A whole lot of photos, apparently taken over half of Europe and with many different men. The photos look like they were taken in secret. There are also some files on the Crystal Spa, but they don't look to contain anything that isn't common knowledge. And there's a report from the *Courier*, only a few weeks old, about a proposed new suburb near Wolfsbach. And a deleted email that could be interesting. Good luck!"

As soon as Tabea had left, the two investigators bent over the computer, excited about what the memory stick would have on it. First, they opened the email that came from an MCM. Tabea had been right – it couldn't have been more candid, because the text said, "You're going to regret this!"

Doris and Lotte stared at each other.

"Is this finally a lead? Let's have a look at her mailbox to see if we can find any more messages from MCM?"

In fact, there was a free exchange of messages back and forth. When Doris opened the first email it immediately became clear that MCM was feminine, because the person addressed was a Marie-Claire.

"I'll go back to Tina's parents. I'll ask them if they know this girl. From what I'm reading in these emails, she is a deeply committed environmentalist. And here she writes … 'when I'm back in Bayreuth …' or here … 'Regensburg is nice, I suppose, but I like Bayreuth better' … I wonder if she lives in Regensburg? Oh well, we'll clear that up later. For now, we'll have a look at the photos."

Many of the pictures showed Tina, all dressed up and stylish in various places right across Europe: Brandenburg Gate, Cologne Cathedral, Munich Hofbräuhaus, in Germany, but as well, the Trevi Fountain in Rome, the Rialto Bridge in Venice, the Eiffel Tower in Paris etc., etc., etc. The girl in the photos looked quite different to the young woman who they had found in the Dammwäldchen. Doris pointed to one of the pictures.

"Look, Lotte. On the one hand she looks like she's just stepped out of a fashion magazine, quite in the world of the rich and the glamorous. But, on the other hand, you can see that she doesn't feel absolutely comfortable in her skin, as if she had slipped on fancy dress. Whatever the reason she was doing it, it was only show, it wasn't the real her. Let's have a look at the other pictures."

As Tabea had said, there were a lot of pictures that looked like snapshots taken in haste and in secret. Some were of Tina with clearly older men, who you could see were dripping in money, while others were of just the men, often in expensive locations but often in equally expensive hotels. Lotte had turned pale and looked at her boss with sadness.

"She looks to be working as a prostitute, that's what it looks like. Oh God, isn't it weird when it's someone you know."

"Well, Lotte, that's life, I'm afraid. Bad things don't only happen to others, they can happen to someone you know. Anyway, this has given us a hell of a lot of work to do. We have to find out who these men are. In theory, at least one of them will provide a lead, and as long as we don't have anything better … But look, there are even more photos."

A short moment later Lotte gave a half-strangled squeal, because in one of the pictures was none other than her beer festival acquaintance from yesterday.

"Bertie? I can't believe it."

Anyhow, it wasn't one of the sinister hotel pictures but a completely normal photo that showed Tina and Bertie, apparently a selfie taken in a beer garden.

"Well, Lotte, you now have an official reason to investigate him. We have to clear up the identity of all these guys, so you can do no better than start with him. At least we know he comes from Bayreuth. Are there any more photos of him?"

There was only the one picture of Bertie, except there were also a few photos of the guy both of them had seen at the beer festival. Doris pointed to the man with the striking combination of an Elvis quiff and a ponytail.

"Look, Lotte. You saw him as well, didn't you? That was the guy who your Bertie went to the carpark with. I'm telling you, something's not right about these two, they've got something to hide. In any case, we need to thoroughly check them out. Get started right away and run them through facial recognition. Perhaps we'll be lucky, and they will be in the database. In the meantime, I'm going to go to Tina's parents and see if I can find out anything about this Marie-Claire. And perhaps the mother or Anna knows these guys."

35

There were hardly more than a couple of trees between them and the mill when Albert abruptly stopped. Lisette looked at him questioningly, and when she saw the expression on his face she became fearful and anxious. She had never seen her brother so openly angry. She hardly dared breath, let alone say anything to him. The horse, snorting and steaming, waited patiently for them as they sat like that next to each other for several minutes.

Finally, Albert spoke – and his tone of voice was at least as cuttingly cold as the persistent east wind, asking, "And? What do you want to do now?"

Lisette glanced at him, disconcerted. She had no idea what her brother was talking about.

"What do you mean, Albert?" she whispered. For once she was not cheeky and provocative.

Contemptuously, and as vulgar as a stable hand, her brother spat in the snow before he answered her. For Lisette it was becoming increasingly frightening.

"With me. And with the piece of music. What are you up to?"

Her face reflected such complete lack of understanding that he could not accuse her of playacting. Lisette obviously had nothing to do with the disappearance of the music. Albert decided to make light of it.

"I put a piece of music in the piano, a piece that I've attempted and practised secretly when all of you are out of the house. I can't find it anymore and because you are the only person who plays the piano besides me, I had suspected you. You haven't taken it, have you? I've only borrowed it. It's important for me to find it again."

Lisette shook her head sympathetically.

"No, I'm sorry, Albert, but I don't know anything about it. But you say you put it in the piano? Where then? In the strings?"

Albert nodded grimly. If even his sister could immediately think of the hiding place hardly a moment after he had mentioned it, then perhaps it wasn't as secure as he had hoped.

"Then perhaps Schlehmüller found it. Yesterday, one of the keys wasn't working properly and he wanted to check if the hammer had caught. I went into the kitchen to get something to eat because I didn't know how long it was going to take. If he found the music, then surely it's lying on the pile on the little table next to the piano. Have you already checked there?"

"No, I haven't. But if Schlehmüller ..."

Albert did not finish his sentence. He thought it was highly unlikely the music teacher would not have noticed the music or, indeed, would not have had a go at playing it. In that case, Schlehmüller would have also read the dedication. And the stupidest thing would be if he had then put two and two together.

Albert suppressed the impulse to turn round on the spot and confront Schlehmüller, but his first priority was to prevent Lisette having suspicions. So he set the horse trotting and steered the sleigh towards the estate. Lisette remained *silent next to him, and he continued to brood. How would Schlehmüller know that S.W. was not a relation who had signed a present? After all, the music could just as easily have been bought. Perhaps Schlehmüller had thought nothing of it but in fact laid the piece on the music pile. Perhaps not even on top so it did not get mixed up when Lisette picked up her own music? That was possible. He knew from his own time as a piano student that Schlehmüller was always careful to put the piece of music that was being played on top. The other pieces found their way down in the pile. Perhaps he was in luck and that was exactly what had happened. It had not occurred to him to search through the pile of music. He would check later.*

At last, he could breathe more easily, feel calmer looking to the future. How good it was that he had not told Siegfried anything; it would have only upset him unnecessarily.

36

Doris Lech was sure of it. The man in the photo was the visitor they had made up an identikit picture for, the guy who had been interested in Tina's computer. But why the interest? Was he only concerned about the photos taken together or was he after something else entirely? Had the files dealing with the Crystal Spa or the newspaper report about the Eierberg something to do with him? Was he connected with this Marie-Claire or she with him? What should Tina regret? There was riddle after riddle that Doris was determined to solve.

She pressed the doorbell vigorously. Frau Hermann opened almost immediately, and Doris was sure that she had already been seen.

"God Bless You, Madame Inspector." Neither the greeting, the unfamiliar Bavarian equivalent of 'Good Day', a strange hangover from more religious times it seemed to Doris, nor the formal mode of address, were what Doris was used to. She did not answer in kind.

"Good day, Frau Hermann. I still have a few questions about the man who visited you yesterday. Can I come in?"

Tina's mother stepped aside without a word and let Doris step in. As she was heading for the living room, Frau Hermann pulled at her sleeve and suggested they go into the kitchen.

"I have to prepare lunch and I can make us some coffee at the same time. You would like a coffee?"

Of course Doris would like a coffee. The offer was clear enough despite Frau Hermann's thick Bayreuth dialect. A few minutes later she was sitting at the kitchen table, a copy of the North Bavarian Courier lying beside her and a large mug of milk coffee in front of her. Without saying a word, she laid the photo on the paper. Frau Hermann, who was sitting on the other side of the table peeling potatoes, stopped in surprise.

"That's the man who wanted Tina's computer. You found him quickly enough!"

"Tina had saved the picture on her hard drive. Apparently, at least in regard to this single point, he told the truth; they did know each other. Frau Hermann, you really have no idea who he could be?"

The woman sadly shook her head and wiped a tear from the corner of her eye.

"It is really pitiful that we knew so little about our daughter, don't you think? I mean, she was our child, she lived here, but we didn't know anything about her group of friends. I think she was ashamed of us. We simply weren't good enough for her friends. I mean, Tina always had herself picked up diagonally opposite us, in front of the big mansion. It made a better impression than our old housing estate place. You know, things have always been tight with us. My husband has often been unemployed. I inherited the house from my grandma, which I am very grateful for, but we've never had enough money to renovate. That's obvious enough, inside, and out. Well, one time I followed Tina, making out that I had to pick up a package from the pharmacy. I watched as she stood in front of the mansion. A red sports car came by, a bright red one. The man driving, he suited the car perfectly. It's quite possible it's him in the photo. I don't know, despite the flash car and the flash driver, Tina didn't look really happy. In fact, she looked more annoyed than anything, as if the last thing she wanted to do was go off with him."

Doris picked up the mug but then put it straight down again because the coffee was still too hot. She jotted a few things down.

"Frau Hermann, I know that it is a difficult time right now, but I have to ask this question. Is it possible that Tina was working as a prostitute?"

In shock, Tina's mother let the half-peeled potato fall. It hit the tile floor with a dull thud and rolled unobserved in front of the sink.

"Tina? For heaven's sake, no. She was studying. She was going to make something of herself. She was studying law and wanted to become a lawyer. She could express herself so clearly. I mean, for a long time she has worked hard, has been genuinely interested to learn how to write legal documents properly. I mean, just a few weeks ago, she printed something out and left it lying about in the living room. It was a draft for a contract of sale. It had to do with a construction site for a beauty clinic in Fichtelberg, you know, where the Crystal Spa was, the place that burned down. It must have been for some sort of seminar, because in reality nobody is building a beauty clinic there. But it was so clearly and expertly expressed, that it did my heart good to know my Tina could do something like that. And then there was another contract, which was even more absurd, to do with the Eierberg. Do you know it? In Saas? It's not even a construction site. It's a horse paddock and in winter a nice toboggan hill for the children. They must surely have been contracts she wrote for practice."

Doris was madly scribbling everything down. She had her doubts about what sort of practice writing the contracts could be connected to.

"Frau Hermann, let's suppose that this man forced Tina to do things that we don't know about. If that's the case, then it's likely he'll do it again. It is quite possible he will get another happy young girl under his control and destroy her life. Take a moment to remember that somewhere out there is a murderer running around undetected. In case you know something else, however unimportant it may seem to you, let me know. I promise you that Tina's name will not pop up in connection with any sort of scandal or intrigue. I personally think that there could be more to these contracts than is obvious and that Tina could have stuck her nose too deeply into something that she shouldn't have. If you know more about these contracts, then, please, don't keep it to yourself."

"No, I really don't, Madame Inspector. I can't imagine anything like that. My Tina was studying law. She must have written them for her course, as I've already said. And this man – I'm sure there's also an explanation for him. We just don't know what it is. Tina was never on the street, never."

"Frau Hermann, I'm not talking about streetwalkers. There are absolutely, how can I put it, more upmarket forms of prostitution, women as companions for rich men, that is to say, as companions to show off in public. Tina's brand name clothes and her trips away would fit her into this category."

Since Frau Hermann angrily dismissed this sort of speculation as belonging in the realm of fantasy, the investigator drank her coffee, which had by now cooled down a little, and steered the subject towards the email contact.

"Does the name Marie-Claire mean anything to you?"

This question took the wind out of the sails of the indignant mother.

"Marie-Claire, yes, of course. She is a friend of Tina's. They were at school together, but in the senior years Marie-Claire left RWG, that's Richard Wagner Grammar School, Madame Inspector, and went to WWG, the Economics and Science Grammar School, because she wanted to do some sort of specialist course that wasn't offered at RWG. Despite that, the two of them often met up. Marie-Claire is now at university studying biology, I think in Regensburg. Or in Erlangen? No, Regensburg. What has Marie-Claire got to do with the death of Tina?”

“We're just checking over several email contacts on Tina's computer; that's why I'm asking. Has the girl got a last name?”

“Mayer. Isn't that absurd? Such a refined French first name followed by such an ordinary German family name; Marie-Claire Mayer. But she wouldn't hurt a fly, so you can take her off your list of suspects, Madame Inspector.”

Doris dispensed with mentioning the threatening email but instead said her farewells with the standard formula.

“In case something else occurs to you or in case this man shows up again, please call me. Goodbye.”

The door of her red BMW convertible banged shut a touch too loudly, because Doris was angrier than she should have been for someone who should remain professionally objective. In a fury, she turned the motor on and let it roar. She drove off with squealing tyres, caught herself not really keeping to 30 kilometres per hour and let off the accelerator.

“I'm a great role model,” she mumbled to herself. “This all smells of a high-end pimp and, somehow or other, a construction scandal as well. And I have honestly no desire to burn my fingers another time. To have my career ruined once is more than enough.”

37

Albert had leafed through the pile of sheet music twice from top to bottom but had found nothing. He felt himself beginning to panic. Schlehmüller must have taken it, there was no other possibility. He sunk immobile onto the piano stool. Albert's father, the old courtier, by now having returned home, found Albert in this state when he came into the drawing room to treat himself to a nightcap.

"Albert, what's wrong with you?" he asked, irritated to see his son there. He had presumed Albert had gone up to his room long ago.

Albert jumped up in fright, as pale as chalk, with a horrified expression on his face. He could see that his father had yet to learn of his secret and, as a result, make his life a misery. After a short moment of embarrassment, he decided on the spot to come clean.

"Father, I need your help. I have a suspicion that Schlehmüller has stolen something from me."

Zweistein looked at him sceptically. As far as he knew, the piano teacher was a law-abiding, upstanding citizen, and he found it hard to believe what his son was alleging.

"You'll have to be more precise, Albert. Schlehmüller and theft – isn't that a little far-fetched?"

Albert sighed. If he had ever had the slightest inkling that his father would believe him unconditionally, now he knew he was deluding himself.

"What I'm going to tell you now, father, won't please you. But I implore you to simply listen to me and not lose your temper."

Zweistein nodded curtly and Albert summoned up all his courage to tell him the whole story.

"I have a relationship, father, which makes me liable to be blackmailed. The man concerned has sent me a piece of music with a personal dedication written on it. I fear that Schlehmüller found it, since today I noticed it has vanished."

His father stared at him, a blood vessel swelling dangerously on his forehead.

Then he burst out, "The man concerned? Man??? What's that supposed to mean? Does it mean what I'm thinking?"

Albert was fearful of the consequences, but he could see no way out, so hesitantly he nodded. The elder Zweistein raised his hand and gave him a resounding box on one ear. But that was only the first move. He started bashing him as if he had lost his senses. Albert at first lifted his arms to try and protect himself, but suddenly a jolt went through him, and he started defending himself. For the first time in his life, he did not simply let his father's violence go unchecked. For the first time he rebelled.

In the midst of the fight, by chance, Albert's fist caught his father completely by surprise and, even more extraordinarily, in exactly the right spot. The elder Zweistein's eyes rolled, and he started to collapse before Albert knew what had happened. He was able to spring forward and catch his father just in time before he hit the floorboards with a thud. Carefully, he let him slide to the floor and then fetched a cushion from the sofa and laid it under his head. He feared how his father would behave when he came back to his senses.

As it happened, Albert did not have long to wait because the old man was already moaning and moving again. Albert would have preferred to flee right then and there but he did not dare.

Alarmed, he kneeled by his father, who now opened his eyes and reacted completely unexpectedly.

"Albert, you don't need to worry, I'll look after it. Schlehmüller is not going to be your problem. But what you do, in future, you do discretely. I'll make sure that you remain a person of integrity in the eyes of the world. Prepare yourself to get married, even this year, but by the latest, next spring. What you then do behind your wife's back is your business – as long as you take care to produce an heir. Do we understand each other?"

Albert stared goggle-eyed at his father. Then he nodded.

"Then help me up will you or am I going to have to spend the whole night here on the floor."

And so it happened that the next day the elder Zweistein travelled to the district military office and had a private discussion there with a good acquaintance. An envelope, whose contents only the two of them would ever know, changed hands, and just a few days later Rudolf Schlehmüller received his call-up notice.

38

Doris Lech swung into the parking place way too fast. Her convertible came within a hair's breadth of skidding sideways, but she regained control just in time, rapidly decelerated and made a conscious effort to park slowly and carefully. She was still furious about the circumstances surrounding the girl's death. There was obviously a hornets' nest just waiting for her to poke around in and let the next property scandal mess up her career. If only she could stick her head under the bed covers and not have to see or hear anything more. But she knew without a shadow of doubt that backing out was not an option. If the signs were pointing in a particular direction, then that was the direction she had to go in. Of course, she could delegate some of the investigative work to Lotte, which was exactly what she would do in this case.

She ran up the stairs and along the corridor in a bad mood, and entered her office, where Lotte was waiting for her, still in a bad mood.

Lotte looked up at Doris inquisitively.

"Well, boss, what have you found out?"

Doris only responded with an ill-tempered shrug of her shoulders.

"Not as much as I would have liked. I suppose I should start with what I have found out. The guy in the photo is in fact the one who went to the Hermann's and asked about the computer. And this Marie-Claire does have a last name; it's

Mayer, and she is apparently studying biology in Regensburg. But she does come from Bayreuth, which should make it easy to find her. And with a bit of luck, she'll be in Bayreuth at the moment so we can interview her ourselves. I wouldn't like to leave it to another jurisdiction. It's always better when you can get to know suspects personally and can draw your own picture of them.

"Unfortunately, that is it as far as successes go. Tina's mother was really indignant when I hinted her daughter was possibly working as a prostitute. That doesn't fit her view of the world at all. She can't and won't countenance it. And with that she isn't prepared to think along these lines or even to help us identify the men in the photos. It isn't possible so it can't be possible. Her Tina, the girl that she knew, was an upright law student. Nothing else.

"But I did find out something else. Tina had actually printed out sales contracts for this sinister spa block of land in Fichtelberg and also for the Eierberg here in Bayreuth. It's got something to do with the construction of a beauty clinic. Haven't we heard about that somewhere else?"

Lotte's eyes widened.

"Do you really think the contracts are the keys to the murder? Perhaps Tina just needed them for her course?"

"Yes, that's what her mother thinks as well. But I'm not so sure about that. Do you know, I experienced something much the same in Cologne? I had irrefutable evidence of scandals in the construction industry, but they were simply swept under the carpet. In the end it nearly cost me my job."

Doris fell silent and stared past Lotte out the window where a blackbird was hopping through boughs dripping with rain.

"Is that why you left Cologne?" Lotte asked softly.

Doris nodded slowly.

"For that reason and because of a guy who was an idiot. Or perhaps, I was an idiot too, who knows …?"

She forcefully cleared her throat and tried to lighten the melancholy tone.

"And you, what have you found out about this Bertie?"

Now it was Lotte's turn to look melancholy.

"Our techies have found him on Facebook. He's not particularly active and has made an effort not to leave behind any private traces. But we do nevertheless know his whole name. He's Albert Zweistein, like the composer. In one of his profile photos it looks as if Tina and the Bird of Paradise are in the background, somewhere in the sunny south next to an old church."

Lotte turned her screen so Doris could glance at it.

"Well, Lotte – an old church! That is the famous Duomo di Santa Maria Nascente in Milan."

"Sorry, I don't know it. My salary only stretches to a holiday on a farm – my parents' farm in Emtmannsberg," said Lotte with a smirk.

Shaking her head, Doris returned the conversation to the investigation.

"Is this Bertie in some way related to the composer, or is the same name just a coincidence? And what else does he do?"

Lotte became serious.

"You won't believe it – he's a doctor. That would be a perfect match for the beauty clinic, wouldn't it? And he actually is the great-grandson of the composer's sister. Her name was Lisette, and she married a distant cousin, so she kept the name of Zweistein."

"Of course, it used to be usual to marry relatives. That way the money always stayed nicely in the family."

"It is possible she inherited the rights to her brother's famous sonata. He died very young and didn't leave any children behind."

Doris considered for a moment, then nodded.

"Yes, I know the piece too. I've even played it myself."

"What, you too? Here in Bayreuth, it's quite normal, everybody has to learn it when learning the piano, because Zweistein came from Bayreuth. I can even play two variations. That you know it and have even played it is incredible."

"Well, yes, it's also a wonderful piece. I loved it so much that I even learnt it by heart – and for me that's really something. But how come two variations? I only know one."

Lotte shook her luxuriant hair and started on a rambling explanation.

"Have I already told you that I absolutely adore old film music? It's a bit of an obsession of mine. I've got the sheet music for some film scores at home. I prefer to play them rather than classical stuff. Well, my brother is a big fan of Ben-Hur. A little while ago, a remake of the fifties' movie came out and when my brother saw that version, he wanted to see the original. He got hold of an old DVD and watched it with some of his boring old friends on a dreary day when I happened to be not feeling too well and spent the whole day lying around on the sofa. So, I was forced to watch it with them. And what can I say – the main theme of the film music of such a monumental film sounded like Zweistein's sonata. I became curious and googled it. The descendants of Zweistein had sold the rights of the sonata to Hollywood in the fifties and made a killing. And with all the dough they bought a huge slice of farmland around Wolfsbach. You know where I'm talking about, the land that was first meant to be a nature reserve but now has suddenly been rezoned as a development site. And if they develop the land, they can in a strange twist make another killing out of old Albert's sonata."

Doris sighed audibly as Lotte finished speaking.

"Once again a strange rezoning of a parcel of land. It really seems to be pursuing me: 'The Curse of Doris Lech' – shady construction sites wherever you look."

Half confused and half amused, Lotte stared at her.

"And do you know what? That's still not everything. My great-aunt told me that there was a strange story to do with Albert's sonata already doing the rounds in the twenties. And indeed, a lady friend of hers wants to enlist a lawyer to look into the whole thing. It goes like this: her friend's great-aunt, old Frau Hagen, had apparently written a type of confession that was found after her death. In the confession it is alleged that the sonata wasn't written by Zweistein at all but was composed by Siegfried Wagner."

Her boss raised her eyebrows in amusement.

"And these are the sort of fairy tales you while away the long, cold, winter nights in Emtmannsberg with, am I right? Lotte, you can't really believe that. If that were the case, then the whole Wagner clan would have been to court long ago."

Lotte bristled.

"Why it hasn't come out is because there's no proof."

Lotte was offended; she found it almost personally insulting that her boss called her great-aunt's stories into question.

But Doris quickly took the wind out of her sails.

"Be that as it may – we're not really going to get any further with this sonata. We must concentrate on the facts, Lotte. And the only facts we have at the moment are with regard to these documents about the spa resort. Have you found anything out yet?"

Lotte, easily diverted, nodded enthusiastically.

"Yes, and actually, I've telephoned a friend of my middle brother's ex," Lotte informed her boss. "The friend's name is Peter," she added, responding to Doris' warning glance.

"How good that in your everybody-knows-everybody-else cosy little world names still exist," Doris commented sarcastically.

"Well, should I now say what I've found out or not? Okay, Peter is a good friend of a local affairs reporter at the Courier, who lives nearby. In any case, he said that the baths operator, Steinhart, was fined by a court for misappropriation of funds and had to pay a million euros compensation. Some of this money went to the municipality of Fichtelberg, while another part corresponded to the worth of the block of land, whose owner is Crystal Spa Limited in Fichtelberg. But there is still a long way to go before it will be built on, and Steinhart has passed away in the meantime. What the subsidiary company of Crystal Spa Limited is planning, no one knows for sure. In any case, the fact is that nothing is being built at the moment, the costs of a new complex are getting higher and higher, and besides there is interest coming from a couple of parties for the undeveloped blocks of land. My brother Florian and this Peter guy, they often go mountain biking in that area and when they were recently whizzing through Fichtelberg, they saw some men quite conspicuously looking the area over. After that, Peter, a reporter in heart and soul, tried to find out straight away what was going to happen in the near future regarding spa resorts and tourism. But no one could tell him anything more specific. It all seems to be up in the air."

"It's obviously not good for the municipality when nothing happens for a long time. It's a pity. I was up there just recently; it's a beautiful part of the world."

"Well, the real question is whether it makes any sense to rebuild the spa resort. That is to say, whether it would pay off now that a new spa resort has just been built only a few kilometres away in Weißenstadt."

"All the more interesting would be alternatives to a spa resort – a beauty clinic, for example," Doris mused.

Short, loud knocks on the door tore them out of their reflections. Tabea from the KTU, full of verve, ripped the door open, and, equally full of verve, swept into the room.

"Hello. I don't want to disturb your private discussion – you look so lost in thought – and I'm also not so sure if what I have will be of interest to you, but you have to clutch at straws, don't you? And indeed, on the scrap of paper that we found, our graphology expert, Franziska, has been able to decipher the word 'For'. She'll come past in a minute and then she can give you the details."

Doris sighed.

"I really don't know what use the hundred-year-old word 'For' is going to be for us, but all the same, thanks for her trouble."

Another knock at the door, this time softer and more timid, was followed by a young woman coming into the room. She was introduced by Tabea as Franziska Bloch.

"She also works for forensics, and she's really fascinated by different types of handwriting. Franzi has even done a few adult education graphology courses."

Doris Lech looked in gentle amusement from one workmate to the other.

"A real expert! Well, that's great. Okay, Franziska, what have you found out?"

Doris ignored Lotte's indignant grimace. Franziska acted as if she had not detected the irony and answered obligingly.

"As you can see, I have enlarged the scrap of paper. You can hardly recognise the word because the ink is so faded. You have to really look at it carefully to even notice that something has been written there. At least, that applies to the 'F', because the paper is worn and has obviously been handled many times. And besides that, where the 'F' is, the fibre structure of the paper is somewhat thickened on the reverse side. We can conclude from that the page was rolled up. Still, the 'o' is a bit stronger and the 'r' even more so. Look, can you see how the 'r' is written with more of a flourish? We can tell from that, that the writer was about to write another word. We can also work out from the way the word is written with a flourish that what was being written was very important to the writer."

The graphologist looked up pleased with herself and, indeed, she had succeeded in impressing Doris. She nodded appreciatively.

"Astonishing what you can get out of a small piece of paper. You've really done that with precision and exactness. Thanks very much. What might the author actually have written?"

Tabea butted in. You could notice that she was really fascinated by the story behind the scrap of paper.

"'For' – that is clearly the beginning of a dedication. And you normally make dedications when you want to give someone a very personal present."

"Yes, correct!" yelled Lotte. "I've always made something for my mother for Mothers' Day and I've always written on it: For My Very Best Mum."

"I've even dedicated various things to female and male friends and all of my relations," it then occurred to Tabea. "I've even dedicated a self-made pottery feeding bowl to my guinea pig, Whiskey."

"Whiskey. A guinea pig called Whiskey?"

Nothing more surprised Doris in this town.

"Yeah, on account of the colour. My grandma always muddled it up. She always called it Cognac. She always said, all that mattered was it was something to drink."

"Hmmm, very interesting," murmured Doris.

"What, that the thing that mattered was something to drink? Or that I dedicated something to my guinea pig?"

“Either of them. Let's get back to the thing about friends. It is highly possible that our old scrap of paper was meant for a good friend. Is the writing a man's or a woman's?”

After a short hesitation, Franziska spoke up.

“Well, in my opinion, a man's. But I can't say for sure. It is written in a very old-fashioned style of writing; my bet is the style taught in schools in the nineteenth and early twentieth centuries, and I don't know enough about that to make such distinctions beyond a shadow of doubt. To be certain you'd need to send the specimen to a graphology institute. But my feeling is that the writing has a certain strength and decisiveness. My bet is a man. But I can't guarantee it.”

Doris nodded in agreement.

“As a layperson, I would have said the same. Now we need to clarify two points. Firstly, where is the rest of the sheet of paper, or, put another way, why is this small corner missing from it. And secondly, what does the whole sheet of paper have to do with our murder. At least we can narrow one thing down in light of the style of writing; how old the paper is likely to be. But can we say anything more precise than that?”

She sighed, adding in resignation, “We certainly won't find any expert here in Bayreuth who can obligingly tell us.”

Her workmates, however, all had a completely different opinion, because they called out in unison, “Yes we do!”

Tabea elaborated triumphantly, “After all, we do have a uni here in Bayreuth and I know someone there …”

“… Do you mean the ex of a girlfriend of your sister's? Him, what's his name again? Stefan, Steffen?” Lotte interrupted, and Franziska answered with a broad grin.

“Stephen, you mean him, don't you? Wow, he's so cool! I'll absolutely have to come along when you take him the corner of paper.”

Doris could only roll her eyes. Evidently everyone really did know everyone else here in Bayreuth.

She could not resist adding, "I hope that he and the girl-friend parted on good terms so that our piece of paper doesn't go up in smoke."

Tabea dismissed her concern.

"Ah, not at all. He's a professional. Come on, Franzi, we'll call him straight away."

39

"And the two of us will look into this friend, Lotte, the one who parades around like a bird of paradise. Have you discovered anything?"

Lotte nodded eagerly and typed on her computer.

"Yes. Look. Here he is. Likewise appearing on Facebook. Phil Kill is his name there. Well, I wonder with a name like that he hasn't been blocked already. He evidently has connections abroad and is active in the fashion industry, if what it says in his profile is even remotely true. Unfortunately, you can't be certain. I only hope that the lure of the memory stick works, and we can find him that way. It's the first time we've used this tracking software."

"Let's hope for the best. We can't change anything now; either it works, or it doesn't. We'll just have to wait. But in the meantime, we can do some more investigation into matters connected to construction sites. Perhaps there is a connection between the Crystal Spa, the Eierberg and the planned housing development in Wolfsbach? Lotte, can you look into that? And we'll call on your Bertie, preferably together. Otherwise, he'll stare deep into your eyes, and you'll promptly forget the whole murder case," Doris concluded jokingly. "Besides that, is there anything else that could be of interest for us in the retrieved files?"

Lotte wrinkled up her nose as she concentrated on the search.

"Here's something else – a video. Let's take a look."

The two of them watched in surprise because the main focus was on none other than Albert Zweistein, alias Bertie. You could only see him from behind. He was sitting at a grand piano. Above the piano framed sheet music hung on the wall. And he was unmistakably playing the Zweistein Sonata. Doris whistled softly through her teeth.

"Look – he's playing a serenade for Tina. His great-uncle's sonata. Lotte, I would keep my hands off that guy, because firstly, he's a complete show-off, and secondly, I'm convinced he's not completely kosher."

Lotte flared up.

"How do you know that?"

She went deep red. It was obvious that she liked him more than was good for an objective investigation.

"People who are not head-over-heals in love call it instinct. Or gut feeling. Or intuition. But the hormones cancel out insights like that."

Doris quickly changed the topic.

"Are there any more files?"

Lotte searched on, her head bowed. It was embarrassing that her boss could see through her so easily.

"Here is something else. An audio file. Shall I?"

"Of course. Let's hear what Tina deleted."

Once more a piano playing a melody could be heard, not as smooth as Albert's sonata, rather unpractised and clumsy. Sometimes the playing stopped and went back two or three bars. Then it became more assured, quicker and more expressive. Lotte jumped up.

"Doris, do you recognise it? That's also the Zweistein Sonata! But the beginning is completely different. Listen, now it's being played again … can you hear? … that sounds … much more melodic, much more harmonious. As if it belongs to it. Ohhh, it's so beautiful! It's going to make me cry."

Doris was as perplexed as her assistant.

"Lotte, what the hell? Listening to it and comparing to the sonata, the one we've played – it's as if someone has drawn a curtain from a mirror, as if we can see it clearly for the first time. In this case, hear it clearly. It's simply brilliant! It sounds as if our sonata was a first attempt and the one here the triumphant final version. Did Zweistein write this as well? And why on earth didn't he publish this version? It's way better!"

Lotte thought hard for a moment and then blurted out, "Boss, suppose that the old rumour is true, that the sonata was actually written by Siegfried Wagner. And suppose further that he, for some reason, dedicated it to the first Albert. And then suppose the first Albert plagiarised it and published the plagiarised version. And suppose yet further that the little scrap of paper with the 'For' is a corner of the title page of the sheet music where the dedication was written. What if Tina had the original and had to die because she had proof of the fraud? Perhaps someone wanted to get hold of this dedication? In the end, someone from the Wagner clan?"

She was as excited as a schoolchild and actually began to drum restlessly on the table with her fingers. But Doris only shook her head sceptically.

"Lotte, what a fertile imagination you have! You'll end up running up Green Hill and arresting Katharina Wagner for me – what a load of rubbish! What reason would the Wagners have to murder for this dedication?"

Lotte again wrinkled up her nose as she searched for an answer to this question. Finally, something occurred to her.

"Well, if something was perhaps going on between Siegfried and Albert? And they're afraid it might come out at long last, and they want to hush it up."

Now Doris couldn't stop herself from laughing out loud.

"Lotte, I had only been here a few weeks when even I found out that it was general knowledge that Siegfried Wagner was gay and had had several homosexual affairs. Do you really believe that would be a reason for murder? No, your imagination is getting the better of you. Come up with a believable argument and I'll book an appointment with Frau Wagner. But not nonsense like this."

Deeply hurt, Lotte twisted her face.

"Only because you want to blame it on Albert. That's what it looks like to me."

"No, Lotte. I certainly don't want to blame it on him. But the fact remains that as well as the strange Phil Kill, he had contact with the victim, which up to now you can't claim about the Wagners."

Presumably Lotte would have sprung at the face of her superior had there not been a knock at the door at that moment and Tabea had not come back in.

"It's me again – unfortunately Stephen had already left for the day. I'll try again first thing tomorrow morning. Nevertheless, there are some new developments. We've now examined Tina Hermann's clothes and found traces of DNA, several different ones, and besides hers they are all masculine. Up to now we can only allocate one to a source, and, in fact, to this hair, that you had bagged. Direct hit!"

Lotte barged in.

"Hair? What sort of hair? I don't know anything about a hair. Boss, did you forget to tell me?"

Doris felt how her cheeks flushed slightly.

"Ah, Lotte, that was actually more of a shot in the dark. The hair came from your jacket, the one you wore to the beer festival. And it wasn't long and curly but short and light. Who did we snuggle up to yesterday? With Bertie perhaps?"

Lotte stared furiously at her colleagues.

"But that's just … the hair could have come from anyone in the crowd. It proves absolutely nothing. Of course, Bertie put his arm around me. It's still allowed, isn't it! But to pluck a hair from my jacket to put a noose around his neck, that's really unbelievable."

Furious tears forced their way into Lotte's eyes, and in that moment, she would have desired nothing better than to be up and gone.

Doris smiled sadly.

"Nice image of the hair and the noose, Lotte. I do know it doesn't prove anything. But if we are honest, then it's undeniable that Tina and Bertie knew each other well. He is one of the few firm leads in this case. A great deal is still pure speculation and in order to change that we will have to interview him. And together. Lotte, I value you and your work very much, but one way or another the feeling has stolen over me that you can't be completely objective when it comes to this Bertie. So, I'm going to come with you."

Lotte found it hard to stop herself from stamping up and down like a small child. She went to the window and looked out to get herself a bit more under control. Despite that she listened intently to what Tabea still had to report.

"Well, there were naturally DNA traces from Tina on her clothing, everything else was a bit strange. Traces of a new synthetic drug were found by the analysis of her hair. Not a lot, but she appears to have occasionally consumed the stuff. It's not very widespread yet, but it is nevertheless a new drug that had spilled over the Czech border. What's more, the pathologist, Dr Kauper, she wants to come and see you."

Lotte pouted her lips.

"Oh well, the girl took drugs as well. Perhaps she was simply being treated by Bertie? Did you consider that? I'm telling you – the doctor is a false lead. I'm going to go to my great-aunt and ask her about the sonata. THAT is a hot lead."

She wanted to rush out, but Doris held her firmly by the arm.

"Not so fast! Firstly, we have to agree on what we are going to do, and I don't agree with you making up your own mind about what you're going to do. Secondly, later on we're going to go and interview Albert Zweistein junior. And thirdly, your great-aunt lives in Emtmannsberg, doesn't she? If you want to interrogate her, then do it this evening after work, that saves having to go there and back during the day. Just leave work half an hour earlier. That'll be fine."

Lotte unwillingly let herself fall back into her desk chair. She continuously rolled back and forth on the chair, gradually getting on Doris' nerves. Nevertheless, she said nothing to her assistant because she could well understand that Lotte was angry and hurt.

Tabea breathed in deeply to demonstrate that she had more still up her sleeve. Having thus regained the attention of the two investigators, she continued her report.

"Franziska has also done some training, connected to work this time, not with adult education, on what psychological inferences you can make from handwriting. And in a note in Tina's purse something struck her –"

"A dedication to her grey hoodie? Ah, it doesn't matter. What struck her?"

Tabea forced a weak smile.

"Franzi needs to join us to explain it herself. She's been held up because she wanted to get a coffee from the vending machine."

Tabea had just finished when there was a knock on the door and Franziska came in holding a paper coffee cup in the tips of her fingers.

"Hello, ladies! Has Tabea already told you about the note? She has? All right. What was interesting was that the note was by itself in a compartment of Tina's purse. So, not just stuffed in anywhere, but put in by itself quite deliberately, like a lot of people carry around photos of their loved ones in a special compartment of their purses. There was something written on the note, 'Only one year!' Judging by the way the handwriting slopes and how the pen has been guided, the note was in the shape of an anchor – indicating a promise or a firm resolution, a type of deadline you set for yourself. But a line has been drawn through the writing with another pen, hard, as if done in despair, as if it hadn't come true, or that she had given up on the resolution."

Doris nodded in appreciation.

"And you worked all that out from just three short words and a line through them – well done. Perhaps I should do training like that sometime."

Franziska swelled with pride at the praise.

She hurried over to Doris' desk and explained.

"It's really not that difficult. Simply put, there are certain regularities from which you can draw conclusions. Here, for example, here you've written 'Bayreuth'. And just from how hard you pressed, or rather, didn't press when you wrote it, you can conclude a certain despondency when you wrote it."

Doris closed the file in irritation.

"I can see I must securely file away all my handwritten notes or else you'll analyse me to death. But what really interests me is why someone would stick a note like this in their purse? I liked the business with the anchor."

Tabea butted in.

"Well, I've got a saying in my purse from a fortune cookie. Written on it is 'A golden sunbeam follows every shower of rain'. I find that beautiful. It's my motto. And an anchor, too, when I'm feeling bad because everything is going badly."

Lotte rolled her eyes, but Tabea did not notice.

"Exactly, an anchor, like on Tina's note," summarised Doris. "Now all we need to know is how old the note is. Can you work that out?"

Franziska shook her head.

"Not really. What we can say is that it isn't old, because it demonstrates too few signs of use. On the other hand, it was stored in a completely separate zippered compartment so it was protected from being damaged?"

"Which increases its importance," threw in Tabea. "I have a compartment like that, and I put my lotto tickets in it."

Doris laughed.

"Just don't let Franziska see them. She'll be able to work out your most secret wishes from the way you make your crosses."

"No, unfortunately I'm not able to do that. But next month I'm going to do more training," said Franziska, voicing her thoughts without noticing that Doris had made a joke out of it.

"Franziska – oh, forget it. You're not going to be in any danger for the next couple of weeks then, Tabea. You can play lotto without worrying," Doris chuckled.

Only now did Franziska realise she was being sent up.

"Oh no, you're making fun of me – if the murder of Tina Hermann is solved because of my help, then you'll see what I'm worth," she grumbled.

Nevertheless, you could see that she wasn't really offended by the joke.

Lotte, who was becoming more and more irritated watching all this, now stood up without hesitation and declared, "All right, that's enough for me for now. If I can't go and see my great-aunt now then at least I'm going to lunch. My stomach is growling like a wolf."

Doris only curtly nodded to her.

"But please be back at the latest in an hour, so we can go visit Dr Zweistein together. Okay, so let's just clear up the loose ends. What else personal was in Tina's purse?"

"Only a holiday photo of the whole Hermann family, that is, Tina, Anna and their parents. Looks like a picture postcard sort of holiday spot, the Chiemsee in Southern Bavaria, or somewhere similar. It's relatively new, I'd say from last year. Everyone looks pretty relaxed and happy, a harmonious holiday, I would say, as much as you can tell from the picture.”

“And Tina's Facebook profile? Have you found out anything there, Tabea?”

Tabea looked guiltily at the floor.

“We haven't looked at it yet. I'll do it straightaway.”

“And I'll help you. Perhaps I can make some deductions from how she expresses herself.”

40

Tabea and Franziska hurried to go out and, as they opened the door, nearly ran into Dr Kauper, who was arriving to deliver her report. With a perfunctory 'hello and goodbye', they ran past her. Even without a training course it was clear to Doris that the three of them knew and understood each other well.

Doris greeted the doctor with a formal, "Good day, Dr Kauper."

Then she noticed a movement at the open door and raised her eyebrows in surprise as she saw Dr Kollrab come in, adding quickly, "And Dr Kollrab. I hadn't really expected to see you now."

Dr Kollrab smiled in embarrassment.

"It wasn't exactly planned that way, but I found the circumstances of the case so intriguing that I couldn't help but seek Klara out in the Department of Forensic Medicine in Erlangen. Admittedly, Erlangen isn't exactly nearby, but I thought the case warranted the trip. I hope it's all right with you that I've come along too?"

Doris nodded, even though a little irritated by the presence of the amateur pathologist. He seemed quite ludicrous, however … not unpleasant. She pushed this thought determinably aside before she had finished thinking it and turned to Dr Kauper, who was holding her hand out in greeting.

Dr Kauper immediately let it be known that she did not hold with traditional German formality.

"Just call me Klara, please. We'll certainly cross paths a lot, so no need to be so formal," she suggested.

Doris was more than happy to comply.

"Doris. And when we've solved the case, we can go and have a drink together … and toast informality, what do you think?"

"Might I, if you are so good to grant my request, be the third in your confederation," added Dr Kollrab. "Rainer."

Doris noticed that her cheeks flushed, and she was angry with herself.

"Rainer, how colourfully expressed," she responded, rescuing herself from her embarrassment.

He had, however, obviously not noticed either his own pomposity or Doris' discomfort, answering unabashed, "Yes, yes, there is something fascinating about informal friendship. But now we want to let Klara have the floor: she also has something fascinating to report."

While Klara busily fetched thickly typed pages out of her briefcase, Doris managed to steal some time to examine Rainer Kollrab. His hair, speckled with grey, was somewhat sparse, but the many laugh lines around his eyes lent him a youthful look, making him look younger than he actually was. A rounded beer belly hung a little over the belt of his pants. In stark contrast, his fingers were long and skinny. His ice-grey eyes sparkled full of enthusiasm. You could see in his manner how much he enjoyed his involvement in murder investigations. Doris could not figure out exactly what it was; there was something about the emergency doctor that drew her to him. With difficulty she tore her gaze away and made an effort to concentrate on Klara's comments. She did not need to try too hard, for her full attention was quickly brought back to the matter at hand after only a few sentences. Klara had really surprising things to say.

"I wouldn't actually be in Bayreuth at all, but after finding out about a lecture on toxicology that's taking place in the Botanical Gardens today, I couldn't help myself. As a supplement to our investigations, so to speak."

Doris was not sure what Klara was getting at.

"That's good, I read about the lecture in the paper, but what does it have to do with our case?"

"Well, hold onto your horses – the lecture deals with, among other things, the poison arrow frog, and our victim was poisoned with a concoction of various frog poisons; a truly deadly concoction."

This news was a real revelation to Doris. She let herself slump into her chair fully forgetting to offer her guests a seat at the same time, and asked after a short reflection, "I've never heard of anything like that before – how do you get hold of something like that? Or can you mix it up yourself? And I've yet to have anything to do with poison arrow frogs, at least not in the course of my work. After all, I'm not Inspector Barnaby from Midsommer Murders. In a private capacity I've seen some displayed in terrariums. Pretty, colourful little animals, but very dangerous. And since they're protected as an endangered species, I know you have to register them if you want to keep them. Personally, I wouldn't want to keep one – although they're considerably more attractive than the bird eating spiders that you can also see displayed like that."

Doris was aware she was digressing and paused. In so doing she caught herself glancing quickly at Rainer Kollrab. He was calmly examining her with his grey eyes which made her quickly look away. Found out, she thought to herself. But it was not clear to her if by him or by herself.

Klara Kauper had obviously not noticed anything because she blithely went on, "To answer your question, if you have the necessary criminal intent you can order a concoction like that relatively easily on the dark web. But it's also conceivable that someone could mix it up themselves. And keeping a small frog like that in a terrarium is not against the law. With a bit of expertise and skill you could extract some poison. Then you could make up a small poison dart and lie in wait and – kaboom! If it hits its target, that would be all it would take."

Doris gaped open-mouthed in surprise.

"You mean, the culprit has done something like dipped a dart in a mixture of poisons from this and that frog and then spiked the deceased in the neck?" she asked, nonplussed.

Klara nodded, adding, "Put simply, you could express it like that. Incredible, isn't it?"

"Unbelievably ingenious," threw in Rainer Kollrab and looked Doris in the eye as he spoke. Once again, her cheeks flushed and although she knew very well that he meant the culprit, she felt a momentary thrill in her stomach. Peter had never been so forgotten about as at this moment in her office.

"Yes, really unbelievable," she murmured. "Are there any other bits of information? Tabea said something before about drugs. How does that look?"

"Yes, there's something in that. The deceased had clearly been consuming a new synthetic drug, but not regularly, just occasionally. She was no genuine addict; the amounts found were just too small – more sort of on the way to dependence. Besides that, we're dealing with a young woman who was very fond of men, to put it discreetly."

Doris sighed.

"Yes, we already knew that. And we put it a little less discretely. She was a high-class call girl."

She was mildly amused to notice that this time it was Rainer Kollrab who went red. She had thought him more mature. To help him out of his embarrassment, she talked on quickly, "There's a scribbled note we found in Tina's purse that I can't get out of my head. 'Only one year!' was written on it. That sounds like a plea to hold on. Perhaps she was being blackmailed?"

Klara considered this information for a brief moment. Then she answered, choosing every word with care.

"That could definitely match what we know. Her hair had been dyed blonde, but she had only been doing it for half a year. Naturally, she dyed it at regular intervals, but the first time was in April. Perhaps something happened then that changed Tina's life fundamentally."

"She seems to have got to know this Phil about that time. And according to her family, she left her old life behind relatively suddenly and started to lead a double life. What did he blackmail her with? And what was going to end after a year?"

Rainer Kollrab cleared his throat and tossed in, "And what did she blackmail him with?"

Doris stared at him confused.

"You mean …? She had a card to play against him in her hand? And the motive lies buried there? That's a very interesting line of thought."

He smiled at her, full of warmth.

"Sometimes things like that come in pairs. And motives seldom exist in isolation. What has this Phil got to say about all of it?"

"Not much yet," sighed Doris. "We have to find him first. But that should be relatively easy because we put some tracing software on a USB flash drive that he picked up from Tina's mother. He wanted to get hold of some photos, so we obliged him. Now we only have to wait till he uses the flash drive. But until then I've got something else to do. I'm really sorry. I wish I had more time for the two of you, but I still have two interrogations for today on my list."

Klara nodded.

"I have to get to the Botanical Garden, in any case, otherwise I'll be too late for the lecture. It was nice getting to know each other. Ciao."

The doctor went out and Doris suddenly found herself alone in the room with Rainer Kollrab. For a moment she had the feeling that the air was too heavy to breathe, but then she managed to control herself and declared in a slightly rough voice, "I'm sorry, but I really need to get on. Perhaps we can continue our discussion another time?"

Dr Kollrab nodded, not taking his gaze off Doris.

"I would like that very much. Perhaps this evening over a glass of red wine?"

She smiled sadly.

"I would love to but unfortunately I can't promise anything for this evening. I can't yet estimate how long I'll have to work. It depends on what comes out of the interrogations."

"Well, in case you can manage it – you can reach me at this number. And I like my red wine chilled."

He put a business card on her desk and let her get on with her investigation.

41

Margarethe had packed the valuable sheets of music into her school bag. She could hardly wait to actually play the piece on the school piano and so hear for the first time what she had already heard over and over again in her mind. For the first time she would find out if the piece actually sounded how she had pictured it in her imagination.

She restlessly slid back and forth on her classroom seat till at last the bell for the end of the school day sounded. Of course, she could just go home with Lisette like most days, but today was relatively warm and dry, so she was happy to go the long way home on foot.

But how frustrating. Before she could be permitted to go to the piano, Fräulein Schmittig required her to attend the first costume rehearsal. Margarethe was not going to perform in the piece as an actress, but that did not stop her being required to wear one of the standard costumes, that is to say, a long dark woollen skirt and a white blouse with a sailor collar. Margarethe unwillingly tried the things on, impatient to get it over and done with so she could at last hurry to the Blue Grotto and sit herself down at the piano.

Finally.

Like a good girl, she began by practising 'Liebestraum' for the school concert, but the instant she was sure she was alone in the school she took out the secret score and played. The room filled with the sound of chords that up until then had *only existed in her mind. The actual sound of them was even more beautiful than she could have ever imagined. She practised oblivious to the world, forgetting space and time. Only when it began to grow dark did she jump up startled, pack her things together and set off on the way home ...*

42

Doris parked her BMW in the carpark of the medical practice. Lotte, who was sitting next to her, made no attempt to get out, but only stared in fury through the windscreen.

"Lotte, what the hell! Can you please for once try to stay objective? You're coming with me whether you like it or not. We have no option but to interrogate your Bertie. I don't like it either but that's the way it is. We have to do it."

"I can't believe that he can even be considered a suspect. You didn't get to know him at the beer festival. He was so nice and made sure I was okay all the time. He gave the impression he wouldn't hurt a fly."

Doris let out a snort, annoyed.

"If that's the way it is then he doesn't have anything to fear, does he. So, let's go."

Lotte followed her boss and let the passenger door bang shut with a loud thud, making Doris imperceptibly flinch. She nevertheless made sure not to say anything, instead walking with purposeful strides up to the entrance door.

It was closed and even after repeated ringing of the doorbell not a soul stirred.

"Damn it – Wednesday afternoon. I didn't think of that. Most medical practices are closed then. But look, that's interesting – he doesn't look to be accredited as a health insurance doctor because his nameplate says, Dr Zweistein, Private Medical Practice. Well, well, well, he's only a doctor for the rich."

Lotte grumbled something incomprehensible and wrapped herself in icy silence on the trip to Albert Zweistein's old manor house in Wolfsbach.

"Ah, I think we're going to have more luck here," remarked Doris looking at the Porsche that stood in front of the garage. A stern look was needed to get Lotte to climb out of the BMW. She tramped to the house behind Doris like a forlorn poodle.

The doctor opened the door immediately after they rang the doorbell, for all the world as if he had already spied them in the courtyard. Doris examined him quickly – she confirmed he was in fact Lotte's good-looking dance partner from the Bocksrück Beer Festival. Two rows of impeccably white teeth smiled at her. The glance from the bright blue eyes appraised her with interest. Coloured contact lenses was Doris' first thought.

If he was surprised, he did not in the least let it show.

"Lotte – how lovely to see you again! And who have you brought along with you? If you had let me know I could have arranged some nibbles. God Bless You, I'm Dr Albert Zweistein," he announced, turning now to Doris, who was yet again pulled up by being addressed in this odd Southern German quasi-religious greeting.

"Also known as Bertie," Lotte grumbled.

"Yes, absolutely. To my friends, Bertie. To what do I owe this unexpected pleasure?"

Doris straightened herself up and pulled out her service badge.

"Dr Zweistein, we're here in a professional capacity. Can we come in?"

He stepped wordlessly aside and let the two investigators into the hall. As he let the front door close, he said, "Go straight through and take the last door on the right. It's open in any case."

The open door led into the drawing room. While Lotte gazed at her shoes in embarrassment, Doris looked around with interest. Furniture in the Biedermeier style of the post-Napoleonic period stood by the window, but the rest of the room was occupied by a dark-brown grand piano. Hanging on the wall over it was a framed musical score. Curious, Doris stepped nearer to examine it more closely.

"That is the sonata my great-uncle composed just on a hundred years ago. Are you interested in music? Do you know the piece, perhaps?"

Albert Zweistein had stepped next to Doris and was making out as if he were studying the score. It was clear to her that he knew it inside out and he was only playacting. Doris, on the other hand, really studied it carefully. Yes, it was clearly the Zweistein Sonata, and apparently the handwritten original. She nodded and turned to Albert.

"Yes, I do. I have even played it. It's got to be a copy, doesn't it?"

He laughed, but not in a friendly way, more self-satisfied.

"Of course. The ink of the original would have faded after only a short time if it had been exposed to sunlight. But, of course, I possess the original, safely stowed away in my safe. Would you like to …?"

He pointed to the grand piano. Doris did not need to be asked twice. A piece lay open on the grand piano, and it was none other than the famous sonata. Although Doris was a little out of practice, she attacked it with great passion and played it to the end. Zweistein nodded appreciatively.

"Not bad for an amateur. Lotte, would you like to as well?" he asked with a self-satisfied grin. It was clear he wanted to perform it himself and wasn't expecting Lotte to accept. But he had not reckoned on the young woman. Without changing her expression, she went up to the grand piano, sat herself down and immediately began playing. What is more, she did not play the original sonata but the modified film melody, by heart and without batting an eyelid. When the last chord sounded, she turned towards him, briefly nodded, and stood up to go back and stand next to Doris. Zweistein stared at her and then clapped two, three times.

"I'm surprised. I hadn't expected that. But now to business. What brings you ladies to see me? If you remember, it was the first thing I asked when you arrived, but I've yet to get an answer."

Lotte was again overcome with embarrassment. Doris, however, appeared to quite enjoy the situation. She pulled out prints of the photos that had been found on Tina's computer.

"Can we sit down? I'd very much like to show you something."

Without waiting for an answer, she seated herself next to the window and spread the pictures out on the table.

"Herr Zweistein, as you certainly must have picked up from the news, the young woman in the photos, Tina Hermann, was a victim of murder this week. Now, as we have discovered yours truly in the pictures, we've come to the conclusion that you knew each other. Please tell us how you knew her, for how long, and how well. Tell us everything on the subject of Tina Hermann that occurs to you."

Zweistein went a trace paler. He slid onto one of the filigreed stools and reached for the photos.

"Tina ...?!? Ah, yes. A fleeting acquaintance. I met her ... last spring ... at the Rosenau. That was shortly before the Rosi burned down. Since then, we met each other now and again, rather by chance via common acquaintances. Tina ... I wouldn't have known that her last name was Hermann," he lied, unmoved.

Lotte had walked over to the window and took in the grandiose view into the distance, all the while boiling inside.

If it had been up to her, she would not have been present for this interrogation. In fact, if it had been up to her the whole damn interrogation would not have taken place at all.

Doris, on the contrary, was immersed in observing the young man and had therefore noticed the barely perceptible shaking of his head that had accompanied the last two sentences. She was now more convinced than ever that this doctor was somehow tangled up in this murder.

"And this man here? Is he just a fleeting acquaintance too or can you at least disclose his last name?" she asked sharply.

Albert looked her in the face, expressionless, and again the thought passed through her mind that he was wearing contact lenses, because a blue like that was simply unnatural.

"I only know him via Tina. Something with P ... Peter? Patrick? I can't remember."

Doris pushed the next photo over the table.

"You can't remember them, although you were obviously in Paris with the two of them, or is the Eiffel Tower in the background on a photo wall in the Rosi?"

Without deigning to even cast a glance at the photo, Albert answered, "You never went to the Rosi when it was still going, did you? Otherwise, you would know that there was no Eiffel Tower there. And even if there had been – the joint burned down shortly after I met Tina. When then, would we have been able to have this photo taken?"

"Exactly. When? And where? Come on, Dr Zweistein. Work together with us or else I could easily come to the conclusion that you have something to hide."

He frowned.

"Okay, okay. I think Tina was going out with this guy. His name is actually Phil. He's a Facebook friend, where he goes under the name of Phil Kill. I don't know his real last name. He does something in the fashion world, and he used to sometimes take her to Paris for weekends. He actually had the mad idea Tina could model for him in a show. A stupid notion. She was no professional model, I mean, she always sprained her ankles in high heels. On account of that they only went to shows to watch. When he had the idea for this short trip, we were sitting together by chance at the same table. He asked me if I wanted to go to Paris. That was it. Otherwise, I haven't had much to do with him.”

“Hmmm. But you can remember the photo so well that you don't have to look at it.”

Doris structured this sentence quite consciously, not as a question, but as a statement, and Lotte unconsciously clenched her fists so much that her knuckles went white.

“Yes, I can. I don't go to Paris so often that I would get mixed up about something I had been doing there.”

He was not letting himself be led onto thin ice.

“Dr Zweistein, what do you think of when you think of the Crystal Spa?” asked Doris, abruptly changing the subject. This time she succeeded in making the doctor lose his composure at least for a short while. He audibly drew in his breath before he answered.

“What should it make me think of? What anyone could read in the Courier? Burned down several years ago, suspicion of arson, which could never be proved. Years of wrangling between the municipality and the insurance company. The occupier has since died and all plans for reconstruction have been put on ice.”

“And you want to have a clinic built there?”

This time Zweistein really went pale.

“What gave you that idea?” he wanted to know.

“Tina Hermann had documents on the subject of Fichtelberg on her computer. These documents revealed that building a clinic there was at least under discussion. And you can well imagine that we have made enquiries with the municipality.”

Here she was bluffing; the thought had just occurred to her. Despite that, she hoped to take Zweistein by surprise. And indeed, he buckled.

"Yes, it was actually under discussion at one time. But nothing came of it, and I have besides found a considerably more suitable site, namely on the Eierberg here in Bayreuth," he admitted hesitantly.

Doris looked quickly across to Lotte, but she was still looking outside and did not give the impression that she wanted to participate in the conversation under any circumstances.

"Oh, and how concrete is it this time? Everything signed, sealed, and delivered?" Doris asked.

Zweistein shook his head, and this time it seemed with genuine regret.

"No, unfortunately not. At the moment, the area is yet to be zoned for commercial development. And the owner doesn't currently want to sell because he keeps his horses there and wouldn't like to have a big construction site in the neighbourhood. But that's all just a matter of time and the purchase price. And negotiating tactics. I just need to be patient."

Now at last, Lotte intervened.

"Perhaps the owner simply doesn't want to sell? Perhaps he has different ideas about life to you, Dr Zweistein?"

She sounded bitter. That was obvious to everyone present. Zweistein laughed, embarrassed.

"Weren't we on first name terms just a few hours ago? Is all that forgotten so quickly?"

Lotte stared at him, fury and anger in her gaze.

"The man I was on first name terms with last night was someone I believed to be an honest, nice guy. Not someone who is only out for profit and who would walk over dead bodies for it."

"Oh – does that mean you think I'm the murderer of Tina Hermann? That is a bit of a stretch, dear Lotte. You can't convince me without solid arguments, especially if I don't know anything about it myself. Let's stay on first name terms, so I don't have anything to do with the murder."

Lotte glanced questioningly at her boss, and when she inclined her head almost imperceptibly, she relented.

"Okay, you're right. It's difficult for me to investigate the man I was dancing with in a tight embrace last night," she admitted. Especially since I'd like to do it again tonight, and a lot more besides, she added in her thoughts. There was nothing she would rather do than believe every word her Bertie said. One glance from him and she dissolved like wax in the sun.

Zweistein looked at her for a long time in silence, before he murmured, "Yes, I can understand that. I also have a problem with being interrogated by a woman who I actually wanted to ring up this evening and ask if she would like to do something together, someone I would like to get to know better, at a private level, not officially. Perhaps we can start again from the beginning when you two have solved this murder case?"

Doris stood up and quickly gathered the photos back together.

"Dr Zweistein, if anything occurs to you, then please call us. Here is my card with the extension number. I would be very gratifying if you could help us further."

Lotte pulled out one of her own business cards and laid it on the table as well.

He put the cards away and went ahead to the front door, where he offered Doris his hand and looked Lotte deeply in the eyes once more.

"I hope we soon get to meet each other again under more pleasant circumstances," he whispered to her with a wink.

The young woman turned away quickly and got into the car before her boss had opened the driver's door.

"Let's get out of here," she said in a husky voice. "It's scary what this guy makes me feel. I so hope he doesn't have anything to do with the murder, because I go weak at the knees as soon as he looks at me or talks to me. He's absolutely the man of my dreams."

Doris threw her a sidelong glance as she drove off.

"I noticed," she replied tersely.

"It's unprofessional, I know, but I can't help myself. Perhaps I should come off the case and let you investigate with Tabea?" Lotte suggested in frustration.

But Doris dismissed the suggestion.

"What a lot of rubbish. Certainly, you shouldn't meet or interrogate him alone. And it would be sensible if you really postponed your private initiatives till after the culprit is found."

"Whatever you say. I'll at least do my best not to be too biased. By the way, I still have a bone to pick with you about the Wagner family."

"What do you mean?"

Doris had classified Lotte's ideas about the Wagners as so far-fetched that she had completely forgotten the brief spat they had had about them.

"You said you'd give Katharina Wagner a visit if I found a convincing argument that the Wagners could be under suspicion."

Doris rolled her eyes. Yes, the ridiculous theory that the Wagner family itself could have murdered the girl.

"Okay, Lotte, spit it out. What logical argument have you come up with?"

She unconsciously pressed on the accelerator pedal, and Lotte yelled out, "Be careful, you can only go 60 here. Do you know how often people get flashed here? We're not on a pursuit."

"Lotte! Your theory."

"Ah, yes. All right. Let's assume that the sonata was in fact written by Siegfried Wagner and not the first Albert Zweistein. And let's also assume that Tina had in fact found the proof and was blackmailing the Wagners, along the lines of 'you pay me a few hundred thousand euros and I'll give you the sheet music with the dedication', and then assume that they didn't want to pay?"

Doris sighed in irritation. Always these scatterbrained speculations.

"Lotte, to begin with, the Wagners would have been able to go to the police. Secondly, they presumably have enough money to be able to pay in a scenario like this. And thirdly, a decisive reason is still lacking for why all this should still matter after a hundred years."

"But boss!"

Lotte let herself fall back with a whoosh onto the leather backrest of the seat.

"That's as clear as a bell – because of the film music! At the time, the Zweisteins made a small fortune out of Hollywood, because the sonata was used for the marketing of this blockbuster film. And the royalties would in a purely legal sense be part of Siegfried's estate. We're talking about a hell of a lot of money. Well, that's not a motive?"

In truth, it did not sound completely out of the question. Doris eased off the pedal and let her convertible roll onto the side of the road. She pulled on the handbrake and leant over to Lotte. She sized up her workmate with wide eyes.

"Do you really believe that?" she wanted to know.

Lotte shrugged her shoulder blades, completely at a loss.

"I don't know. But it's at least worth considering. It's no more and no less absurd than all the other theories that we've come up with so far. And it fits with the old note."

"I'm not so sure. Yes, it is conceivable. But Zweistein has the more obvious motive."

This remark made Lotte put up her defences again.

"How obvious the motive, and, above all, how important, lies solely in the eye of the murderer. What may seem a trifle to us can be of such existential importance to the perpetrator that for him murder represents the most compelling solution," she explained indignantly.

Doris bit back a smile.

"Lotte, since when do you talk in such a highbrow way? But I have to agree with you, and after I told you that I would make an appointment with Frau Wagner if you could give me a logical basis for why I should … all right, good, I'll ring today and see to it that I can get to meet her as soon as possible. But we've still got something else to do today – Marie-Claire Mayer. Do you want to come, or would you prefer to hold the fort in the office?"

Lotte thought about it for a moment before saying, "If it suits you, I would rather go to the office. We need to see if there is anything new regarding Phil Kill. And then I can get straight onto ringing the Wagners on Green Hill and make an appointment for you with Katharina Wagner, if that seems right by you."

"Agreed. But only if you don't accuse her straight away on the phone of being an accomplice," Doris said, grinning. "Oh, and if you don't find out anything about Phil Kill and as a result have some time on your hands, then you can happily go past Dr Held, the lawyer …"

"… who Tina did her work experience with. I know. No problem, I'd love to."

43

"Who could that be at this time of night?" asked Winifred, betraying a hint of annoyance.

The knocking on the door was insistent and persistent. Little Wieland was already becoming restless in his cradle. It would not take much more, and he would wake up ahead of time and start whining. Siegfried hurried to go to the door and check. He was not exactly delighted when he recognised the evening visitor.

"Albert, what are you doing here?" he hissed at the man standing opposite him. He glanced briefly over his shoulder – fortunately his wife was at that moment bending over the cradle to pick up the infant, who was by now well and truly awake.

"Winnie, it's a business matter. I'm going outside for a moment."

"Put something on, it's cold outside," Winifred Wagner answered considerately before dealing with Wieland.

Siegfried drew the front door noiselessly behind him, grabbed Albert by the arm and walked him briskly a few steps into a nearby dark lane.

"Have you completely lost your senses?" he snarled. "Do you want to ruin us both? I hope it's clear to you that I became a father a few weeks ago. We can't meet as openly as before, and you know exactly how quickly gossip gets around in this backwater."

Albert sighed dejectedly.

"If you didn't make such a fuss then it wouldn't occur to anybody to think anything improper about the two of us. Apart from that I stand by my suggestion. I'd run off with you this minute, it doesn't matter where – Berlin, Paris, Rome, wherever. You were the one who didn't want to."

Siegfried looked at Albert wistfully.

"You know what I feel for you. But I also love my wife and am responsible for her and for my son. I would never leave them, not even for you. Let's just leave everything as it is, making sure we always meet up in secluded locations, and otherwise each living his own life."

Albert's bitter laughter was short and hard, almost like a gunshot.

"Apropos of each living his own life, I too will be marrying in the foreseeable future, since my father now knows about it."

Siegfried went a shade paler.

"About me?" he wanted to know.

Alfred laughed bitterly again.

"Have no fear – as if I would get you mixed up in it. No, he doesn't know your name. But just the fact that you play a role in my life is enough to send him looking for a wife."

"And who is the girl? Do I know her?"

Albert laughed his joyless laugh for a third time.

"As if I would even know who she is. He's looking around for someone, and he won't care much who she is or whether she suits me. All that matters is that it looks good. But I presume such hypocrisy isn't new to you."

Siegfried did not react. He had always skilfully avoided going into details about his family to Albert. Whether and to what extent anyone was told, that had nothing to do with his young lover. Siegfried was sure of one thing – the more details other people knew, the easier you could become the target of malicious gossip and even blackmail. He was not going to cross that line now.

Siegfried growled, "And you've come here to tell me that? Or is there another reason for your unexpected, and I must say, unwelcome visit?"

The boy involuntarily pulled his head in like a scolded schoolchild. It pained him that he had offended Siegfried and at the same time he was aware that his message would hurt him even more. Nevertheless, it was important to him not to leave his lover in the dark about the risk they were now exposed to. As a result, he answered the question honestly.

"Yes, unfortunately there is another reason for my coming. Do you remember the sonata that you gave me as a present?"

"As if I could forget it …"

All of a sudden Siegfried's voice sounded warm and soft, which disheartened Albert even more.

Sheepishly he continued.

"It was stolen."

Siegfried flew into a temper.

"What?" he called out far too loudly. He immediately realised his mistake and drew Albert even deeper into the shadows.

"What?" he repeated, agitated. "How could that happen? Didn't I ask you to store it discretely? And didn't you promise me that if it was ever published it would only be published under your name?"

Albert felt how, like a child, the tears were welling up in his eyes.

"Siggy, I swear to you, I hid the music well. I stashed it in our piano. But my sister's piano teacher, unfortunately for him, found it because it was making a hammer stick.

Apparently, he took it, because since then it's nowhere to be found."

This time it was Siegfried's turn to laugh joylessly.

"And if ... should he try to profit from it. Does he want money for his silence? Good, he can have it. It should get stuck in his greedy throat. Is it fame, to bask in someone else's glory? That doesn't matter either. I can compose new pieces. It's not the end of the world. It's only a pity for you that you lost it. Don't fret, my dear."

Albert sighed.

"Don't worry. My father has now come into play. He made sure the man was conscripted and sent to the front. It seems he was killed a few days ago. But that doesn't help us much. The music is and remains lost. Perhaps it's better that way because if it ever shows up again, we'll have to do everything we can to get our hands on it. You have to promise me that, Siggy."

"Even if I don't think it will ever see the light of day again – who knows where the man may have hidden it – I can promise you with pleasure I will get hold of it. In the end I'm in deeper trouble than you. There are a lot of A's in the world but considerably fewer S.W.'s, at least in Bayreuth. Let us solemnly swear – as soon as we hear where the music might be, we attempt everything humanly possible to get it back."

A short embrace, considerably shorter than Albert would have hoped, and Siegfried disappeared back into the house. When he opened the door, the wailing of the discontented infant carried over to Albert but was abruptly cut off when the door slammed shut. Albert lent against the trunk of an old chestnut tree and gazed with an aching, burning heart at the brightly lit small windows, behind which loomed the silhouettes of his lover and his lover's wife.

'Siggy, oh dear Siggy ...'

At last, in a fury, he pushed himself off the tree and set off for home.

44

Doris Lech's red convertible was a striking dash of colour on a drab, wet October afternoon. Shaking her head in disbelief, she turned off the main road between Mistelbach and Eckersdorf into the State Forest, driving over a wellmaintained gravel road covered in dirty brown leaves shining with damp.

"How on earth can you get a permit to build here?" she murmured to herself.

An official enquiry at the Residents' Registration Office had resulted in Doris finding out that MCM, alias Marie-Claire Mayer, had apparently studied for three semesters in Regensburg but had been living back in Bayreuth since the summer semester. What had happened? Had she dropped out or had she just changed universities? A short telephone call confirmed the latter, that since returning, Marie-Claire had in fact enrolled at Bayreuth University and had moved into a tiny house in the middle of the forest. Just the thought of it was enough to make Doris shudder. She was and remained a city person. Living in a lonely location like this would have made her permanently ill at ease. Who could know what sort of undesirables roamed around the forest at night or spied on the house ready to use any opportunity to break in and rob the place or indecently assault a young woman like Marie-Claire?

She took the last curve a bit too fast and skidded on the wet leaves but got the car back under control and travelled the last few metres somewhat slower. The regular, official driver training she got with the police was worth it, she thought, a contented grin spreading across her face. She parked her BMW in front of the tiny house that was painted a dusky pink, got out and looked in vain for a doorbell. Not even a letterbox was to be seen. What a desolate place! It annoyed her no end. In the absence of a doorbell, she finally knocked firmly on the front door. There was light shimmering from a window under the gabled roof that made Doris confident that she would get to meet the resident. In fact, she heard a staircase creak and then someone called out.

"Who's there? I'm on my way."

The door was ripped open before Doris had time to answer. She stared somewhat bewildered at the person now standing opposite her. She had truly not imagined a girl who was a friend of Tina's would look like this. She had tousled short hair, wore bib and brace overalls under a mottled-grey traditional-style knitted jacket and thick woollen socks but no shoes, or at least, no inside shoes. Doris was in turn being appraised grimly by the stocky young woman.

"Who are you then? I don't give anything to charity, and I don't buy anything sold door-to-door. Goodbye."

Marie-Claire was about to slam the door in Doris' face when Doris, quick as a flash, put her foot in the way.

"Just a moment. I'm from the Criminal Investigation Department. Detective Chief Inspector Doris Lech."

"Anyone can say that," snarled the student, who felt around in the half light of the entrance hall and all of a sudden pushed a shotgun under Doris' nose.

Doris felt herself starting to sweat. At least that was normal. She slowly lifted her hands.

"Listen. I've got my service badge in my right back pocket. I will now reach in and bring it out. Okay?"

Marie-Claire nodded reluctantly.

"But really slowly, understand? Otherwise, I might get nervous."

So, in slow motion, Doris fished the ID out of her pants pocket and held it up to the girl.

"And now put the shotgun down, otherwise I might start thinking about asking you for your gun licence."

"I'd think twice about that, police lady. There again, I'm sure you're going to want answers from me, whatever the questions might be."

But at least she lowered the barrel.

"Were you just trying to threaten me? But good, let's put the matter of the shotgun aside for the moment. May I come in?"

Without a word Marie-Claire stepped aside, leant her weapon back in the dark corner and went ahead into a small room in which a stove was spreading cosy warmth. A quick flick of the light switch and the little room was bathed in bright light. Again, Doris was annoyed. She had rather hoped to see the room lit up by a candlestick, like in Count Dracula's castle.

"What do you want from me?" Marie-Claire wanted to know.

She let herself sink into an upholstered armchair and pushed a second armchair in Doris' direction. Doris interpreted this as an invitation and sat down as well.

"When did you actually last see your friend, Tina Hermann?"

A contemptuous sound came out of Marie-Claire.

"Bah, that slut – why are you interested in her?"

"They're hard words for a good friend," Doris commented.

She laughed out loud by way of response.

"Hah, don't make me laugh. Friend. What meaning do you attach to the word? She was a friend once, but I'm finished with the traitor. She's dead to me."

"A traitor! Okay … can you explain to me why she's a traitor?"

"I don't know why. I saw her for the last time two or three weeks ago. And now I would like you to leave my house unless you have a search warrant with you."

She stood up with a jerk and motioned with her head in the direction of the front door. With a sigh, Doris got up as well. A sizeable object covered by a large piece of cloth had already roused her curiosity when she came in and now, in one, two rapid steps she crossed over to it and took off the cloth.

"Aha – what have we here? Perhaps I should really come back with a search warrant – who knows what else might show up then? On the other hand, I could plead that I had to carry out a search without a warrant because there was a danger evidence would be tampered with … what's that there on this little sign? Phyllobates terribilis – correct me if I'm wrong, but that's a species of poison arrow frog, isn't it, one of the most, if not the most poisonous species? Which one these colourful little guys is it then? And what are the others called? I would have thought little animals as poisonous as these would be better off living in a zoo than in a little witch's house in the middle of the forest."

Furious, Marie-Claire stood herself in front of the terrarium.

"OK, that might be. But keep your distance. They are mine and they are all, without exception, poisonous."

Doris swallowed down her rising unease. "And let me guess, not exactly legally purchased, are they?"

Marie-Claire pouted, offended.

"What if they weren't – OK, you've caught me. And what now?"

"If I were in your place, I would be more cooperative. It could save you a lot of trouble. I want to know everything about your friendship with Tina."

Marie-Claire sulkily sat back down.

"All right then. I visited Tina just a little while ago. I went to see her about a nature reserve near Wolfsbach. It's a special place where animal and plant species can be found that have become very rare elsewhere, and in many other places are already extinct, and that, when considered from an overall perspective, are severely threatened.

"So, for example, a rare form of marsh orchid is growing in a water meadow there. And you wouldn't believe the animals you can find! The brown long-ear, that's a type of bat. You can also find spadefoot toads there, if you know where to look. And in some particularly clean ponds you can even come across a great crested newt. I'm telling you – it's absolutely worth protecting. Admittedly, amphibians are my passion."

"I would never have guessed that," Doris said with an ironical sidelong glance at the terrarium, but Marie-Claire did not notice.

"In any case, I was able in the past to win Tina over to help me with this project. We wanted the area classified as a nature reserve or at least as a conservation area. You know, I'm not as articulate as Tina, I can't express myself as well as she can. Back in school I always got my As in biology and Tina got hers in German. It explains why she is studying law. In any case, the two of us were really in it together and were close to achieving our goal after weeks of written exchanges with the local nature conservation authority.

"And that was all before my last visit! It was then she told me bluntly that all of the plants and animals were going to die out because the land was going to be rezoned as residential development land. She said she knew first-hand, from the owner himself, Albert Zweistein, who had made an application for rezoning. Apparently, she is a close friend of his and of his friend Phil Großmann, but she refused to introduce me to them. What was the big deal in just helping me meet them; but oh no, the dumb cow simply told me that there was no way she would let me talk to them, or to any other investor, that she couldn't help me anymore and, for that matter, didn't want to.

"When she said all that, well, I completely flipped and really swore at her and stormed out. I mean, I could simply kill her, the traitor! If she'd wanted to, she certainly could have helped me. But no, she had to betray our dream, and all the poor animals as well. Do you know what she said? That it all didn't matter because animals were dying out everywhere because of housing developments. So, now you know everything, even if, I guess, it doesn't interest you much. But why, exactly, are you here?"

A sad smile crossed Doris' face.

"What I'm interested in is your friendship with Tina, your friendship that's now over."

"Has the dumb cow been up to something?"

"Tell me, Marie-Claire – do you read the papers? Or do you now and again listen to the local radio station? Don't you have a TV or at least a computer where you can read what's going on in the world?"

The girl snorted contemptuously.

"Right – so that's it, is it? You want me to register for a TV licence. You're barking up the wrong tree there. I loathe all of that modern stuff. I occasionally use the internet for my course when I absolutely have to. And that's always in the university library."

"Listen, I need to ask you something else. This Phil guy, are you sure his last name is Großmann?"

Marie-Claire nodded vigorously.

"Yes, I am. At least, that's what Tina told me. It would be stupid if I hadn't taken note of the name. I even tried to make a time to meet him and this Zweistein guy to explain to them how important this ecosystem is, but I was straight out turned down."

"Marie-Claire, I also have to let you know something else. Tina is dead. She was murdered."

"Oh, my God. You're not serious, are you? Tell me it's not true. Who would want to kill Tina?"

The girl sat up in the armchair, her eyes wide in horror. She stared at the chief inspector completely at a loss.

The realisation then seeped in, and she whispered flatly, "Good heavens. You think that I … on account of the email I sent her when I was furious with her … but I would never ever … she was my friend, after all … so many years …"

Doris gazed at her with compassion. Did a murderess look like this?

"At the very least, you belong to those under suspicion because of the email, I can't deny that. And your frogs here don't make it any better because Tina was poisoned. I'll go now, but please keep yourself available for us, don't let the frogs mysteriously go missing and don't suddenly disappear yourself. I promise you, if you are innocent, I'll be the last person to report your little zoo."

Doris stood up and went back into the small entrance hall. When Marie-Claire switched on the light, the chief inspector noticed a dartboard hanging at the end of the hall. Interested, she took a few steps up to it.

"So – you play darts?"

Marie-Claire shook her head. If she hadn't been so shocked by the news about Tina's death, she would probably have laughed at this assumption. Instead, she confined herself to a short explanation.

"No, I find darts totally boring. But you know, I'm still hoping that I can get onto the waiting list for Veterinary Science. And as a vet you have to be able to know how to use tranquilliser darts. Therefore, I often practise here with a blowpipe when it's raining steadily outside or something like

226

that. It's actually a lot of fun. If you want, you can have a go too.”

Doris declined.

“And I was worried what could happen to you here in such an out-of-the-way place. That was obviously unnecessary – you give an extremely strong impression of being able to look after yourself.”

“No one comes too close to me, you can be sure of that.”

“And by the way, I do have a firearms licence,” she threw in as a parting shot.

45

Still no trace of the mysterious Phil Kill. Lotte was slowly becoming annoyed with the guy. Why couldn't he just put the stupid memory stick in his computer and let himself be located.

In a fury, she grabbed the note where she had scribbled the address of the building where Dr Held, the lawyer, had his chambers and set off to interrogate him. It was not particularly far from the station, so she decided to walk, a decision she soon regretted, as after only a few minutes she was shivering from a fine drizzle seeping into her jacket. Yes, autumn could be beautiful – when the sun lit up the leaves in all the colours from yellow to red to brown, when nature simply exploded in a rush of colour, but absolutely not when it was eight degrees and raining.

Lotte quickened her steps and was relieved when she saw Dr Held's nameplate. She slipped into the office building and shook herself in a dubious attempt to free her coat of raindrops. She took a quick look at the information panel next to the stairs. Dr Held's chambers were on the second floor and Lotte decided to use the stairs. Surely a little exercise could not hurt and might even warm her up a bit? It turned out a vain hope for she stood a little while later still wet and cold at the chambers' reception desk, rubbing her clammy hands together to warm them up, while opposite her an elderly woman in subdued grey held her service ID in claw-like fingers as she inspected it thoroughly.

"You can see that I'm telling the truth. I *am* from the Bayreuth Criminal Investigation Department. I've a few questions for your boss. Now, if you would *be so kind* and let him know I'm here?"

But Lotte was up against a stone wall.

"It may be that you are from the police, but you still don't have an appointment. Dr Held, on the other hand, does have one. And because that appointment is now and he doesn't want to be disturbed, it's out of the question that I let you see him straightaway. You'll just have to be patient, like every other visitor."

Frau Mauser knew no mercy. On the contrary, she was enjoying the situation. This young thing could not seriously think she could make her own rules. Under no circumstances. It would do her good to quietly twiddle her fingers for a while and wait her turn. Matters were truly going far too far if the young thought they were the only ones with rights. Thank goodness Dr Held had a reliable employee like her. She was, so to speak, the gatekeeper of his fortress, prepared, at the risk of her life, to defend it. Well, perhaps not at the risk of her life, but she would really go to great lengths for her boss.

However, the faithful secretary had not reckoned on Lotte, who had been drilled to prevail over adversity. She quickly had a look around to reconnoitre the layout of the rooms. There was a small seating area in the entrance hall, presumably for waiting clients. Directly next to it was a door standing ajar with a resplendent gold plate announcing 'Meeting Room'. Right behind the reception lady was an open office door, which allowed a view of an empty desk. And next it yet another door, made of dark mahogany, without a sign. At the far end of the corridor was a quite normal door with a sign that Lotte couldn't make out from the other end, but she assumed was the door to the toilet. So, the lawyer's office must be behind the dark mahogany door, and without paying any heed of Frau Mauser's indignant admonitions, she quickly walked across to it and, after a single knock, opened it – coming within a hair's breadth of being hit by a dart that whistled past her head to end up stuck in the carpet of the entrance hall. Lotte blanched.

Dr Held was obviously as shocked at Lotte. With a quick glance, he assured himself that the dart had missed her and landed harmlessly on the floor.

"Oh, dear heavens," he cried, his voice trembling a bit from the shock. "That was close. Please, you'll have to excuse me, my secretary didn't announce you. Normally, I don't try to throw darts at people, you have to believe me. May I ask who I nearly hit?"

Lotte nodded and fetched out her ID. Tiny pearls of sweat sprinkled her forehead.

"Lotte Kerner, Bayreuth Criminal Investigation Department. You might have ended up with me investigating you, Dr Held," Lotte attempted to joke. "Your secretary is in no way responsible. She didn't want to let me through, but I took no notice of her and came in without being announced. You're a good throw."

"That's not so surprising. It's my hobby, you see. Do you want to give it a try before you let me know the reason for your visit?"

Lotte declined.

"No, no. Let's just say I'm a woeful shot."

But Dr Held was having none of it.

"That's not possible. Look, you need to keep your hand nice and relaxed but your body tense. You need to concentrate on the tips of your fingers and keep the target firmly in view – you have to want to hit the target. Determination is half the battle."

Lotte, in fact, did not do all that badly at throwing a dart at the board hanging on the inside of the door.

"Well, see – not so woeful."

Lotte let her gaze glide appreciatively over the cups that were set in a row on a bureau.

"Well, when I see all of them, then I can see that you really are good at it."

Dr Held smiled.

"Well, you know, in my position you have to play golf because of the business contacts that you have to nurture, but my passion is darts."

"And you can determine beforehand exactly where you want the dart to hit and how far it's going to fly?" Lotte wanted to know.

"Well, yes."

Dr Held had a bit of a stretch.

"Naturally, it doesn't always work, but usually there are only small variations – we're talking millimetres here. But tell me … is it Frau or Fräulein Kerner? … you certainly haven't come here to discuss playing darts. I would rather presume it's to do with Fräulein Hermann. It's really unpleasant what happened to her. Such a nice friendly young woman. Are you certain she was murdered?"

Lotte nodded.

"Yes, unfortunately. What can you tell me about Tina Hermann? Did you know her well? What I mean to say is, do you know any relevant details of her private life. Was she perhaps picked up after work by a boyfriend? Or did she now and then let drop a remark about what she had been doing the previous weekend? Things like that would be very informative for us."

"Oh, dear me, where should I begin? She actually didn't give much away. Last spring it seemed she was briefly in love. At least, I presumed that, because she was less attentive than normal and repeatedly made small mistakes. She seemed to be floating on a cloud. But it was soon over. It apparently hadn't lasted long. But after that she obviously changed what she did in her free time because she was often tired, especially on Mondays. There again, she was always wide awake if the topic was the goings on in building projects or the complaints of residents. The Crystal Spa, for example, she was unbelievably interested in that. She wanted to know everything about it. And on her last day here she again listened to me carefully when the topic was the enquiry by old Frau Weigelt."

Lotte pricked up her ears.

"What's that about?" she probed.

"Oh, nothing very important. An old lady claims the Zweistein family has got hold of a large part of her property in Wolfsbach by criminal means. Quite mad. The matter goes back almost seventy years, and she brings it up only now? No sooner is the land rezoned as development land, which is a big windfall for the Zweisteins, than every man and his dog wants to have a piece of the cake and claim to know hidden secrets."

"Actually, I've personally heard of these hidden secrets, as you call them," Lotte said wide-eyed. "My great-aunts talk about these self-same secrets."

Dr Held had to laugh.

"Yes, that's just what you would expect of Bayreuth people. They never forget scandals and unsolved mysteries. However quickly the world may change, these types of myths seem to just about go on for forever here. But wait a moment – Lotte Kerner – are you from Emtmannsberg? Herbert's daughter? Yes, really? He had four sons and two girls, and if you are that Lotte, then you're named after the sister of a friend of ours, whose brother-in-law ..."

"... was killed in an accident in the winter of 1998/99 while collecting wood, exactly," added Lotte. "My father was there at the time. He pulled him out from under the tree trunk, but it was already too late. A sad business. My father often talks about it when he's had one beer too many. And his sister-in-law, Lotte, is often round at our place. She's a good friend of my mother's."

Dr Held thought for a moment and then asked, "Um, Lotte, you don't happen to know how the business with the renovation of the castle is going? It's just that I've heard from a good acquaintance, who you might also know, the godfather of …"

This time Lotte put a stop to it.

"Dr Held, it's really nice to chat with you but I'll have to postpone our conversation until after we've solved our murder case. I also have to talk to your secretary, and I've got a mountain of paperwork waiting for me at the office. At the earliest I won't be finishing work till ten tonight."

He seemed perplexed.

"Ah, well, of course, I won't hold you up unnecessarily, Lotte. But if you have time, get in touch and we can talk about the renovation. Bye for now."

As she went out, she could see out of the corner of her eye that he was reaching for the next dart. She quickly shut the door.

She got nothing out of Frau Mauser, who sat on her chair with a pinched expression on her face and lips pressed firmly together.

"How should I know what that young thing was doing? She never said anything to me. We never spoke privately. Why should I begin a friendship with a work experience student who didn't know anything, couldn't do anything, and didn't want to learn anything? They're all the same. Partying and dancing, that's all they've got in their heads – and men. Once I saw her with one, oh good heavens, he looked absolutely frightful. Like a mad parrot."

In saying this, Frau Mauser rather gave herself away by slipping into the local dialect.

Lotte rummaged about automatically in her bag and got out the photo of Phil Kill.

"Was this the man, by any chance?"

The old lady nodded enthusiastically.

"Exactly. That's him. Gruesome, isn't he? How you can go around looking like that …?"

Admittedly, the guy looked quite exotic, but not, however, as terrible as Frau Mauser made him out to be.

"Anyway, ponytails like this are fashionable. And you often see these Taliban beards on young men. Actually, they don't look so impressive when they're blond," Lotte mused.

"Dear God – are you saying he's a Moslim extremist?"

"Muslim," corrected Lotte without thinking. "And no, I don't think so. It's just fashionable these days to go around looking like that. Can you think of anything else to do with Tina?"

"No, nothing. Apart from one thing. I have my suspicions she tried to poison me."

Frau Mauser lowered her voice for dramatic effect with her last words.

"Poisoned."

"Yes, and do you know why I think so? Because I have worked here now for over forty years and have never, do you hear me, never had even one day off sick. And in her last week working here, Tina made the coffee, and I had such diarrhoea that I had to stay home for two whole days. Can you imagine that? I'd like to know what I'd done to the young thing that she did that to me," she concluded, having worked herself up into a fury.

Lotte looked at her sceptically.

"Frau Mauser, with the best will in the world I can't imagine that to be the case. Why would she have wanted to do something like that?"

Again, the dramatically lowered voice.

"To boot me out. She was keen to get my job. That's the reason why."

"Oh, Frau Mauser. I hope you don't really believe that. Tina was doing law. She could have become your boss at the end of her course. Why would she be keen to take your job off you?"

Lotte shook her head in disbelief. The things people come up with.

Frau Mauer clamped her thin lips even more firmly together and hunched her shoulders.

"I know what I know," she mumbled, making Lotte hurry to leave.

46

It was working a lot better now, the mysterious new piece. It was not just the harmony of the chords or the catchy melody with surprising twists. No, it was also the dark secret that hung over this music that had preoccupied Margarethe for months now. She had given up hope of ever learning anything about its origin, although she was sure her mother knew. Then again, she might someday find out when her mother had gone halfway towards getting over the loss of her husband. Who could know when that might be? But until that day Margarethe indulged in romantic daydreams and made up scatterbrained fantasies about how, from whom, and why her father had come to have the music.

If only he had told her everything. If only he had kept his word and returned unhurt. But all the crying in the world would not help. It was, as it was.

So, at every opportunity that offered itself, Margarethe fled into the school music room, the Blue Grotto, and there in the basement practised the piece that brought her father fleetingly back to her. She had already cried many a passionate tear there but, on the other hand, when she played it she felt him close enough to touch. In her innermost being she was convinced that there was a life after death and that he could hear her. Today, as well, she would stay back alone at school and be able to play the mysterious piece.

Of course, she did not carry the sheet music to and fro every day, that seemed too risky. Rather, after much deliberation, she decided to hide the score in a place where no one would find it. The dark woollen skirt of her performance costume had a small pocket worked into it. On a rainy Friday she secretly took the costume home with her, neatly unpicked the inside pocket, and busily sewed in an old tea towel, in this way enlarging it. No one knew what she had done. No one guessed anything. The old tea towel perfectly hid the valuable sheets of music that she tied up into a small roll with a headband. She could fetch them whenever she had the chance and take them down to the Blue Grotto.

Today, as with other days, just like a good girl should, she practised all the pieces that Fräulein Schmittig had given her and waited patiently until all the teachers had left the school. She finally heard the heavy main gate slam shut and looked out expectantly. The French teacher, Mademoiselle Nicout, had conscientiously locked up and was hurriedly leaving the school property. Margarethe was now alone in the building. Relieved, she rushed across to the wardrobe, quickly glanced over her shoulder to make sure she was truly alone, took out her skirt and fetched the music out of the pocket. As she unrolled the paper, she had the idea that she actually did not need all the sheets, that she at the very least knew the first page off by heart, not to speak of further passages on other pages. Lovingly stroking her finger over the personal dedication of the mysterious S.W. to the beloved A., she felt as if it were a dedication from her father to her herself. No longer needing it to play the piece, she rolled the first page up again and hid it back deep in the folds of her skirt. With the rest of the pages in her hand and a spring in her step, she ran back to the Blue Grotto, excitedly looking forward to completely immersing herself in her piano playing. It did not take long for hot tears to pour down her cheeks at the memory of her dear father. Completely lost to the world, she practised the sonata with such expressiveness that she was certain he would have been proud of her.

Distracted by a fleeting shadow, she glanced across to the ground-level basement window. For a moment that magically stretched out forever, she gazed directly into steel-blue eyes that appeared ready to gobble her up, but at the same time threatened to drown her.

The rest is history ...

47

The rain had got heavier, and the oncoming cars blinded her with their headlights reflecting off the wet asphalt. She hated driving in the dark and the rain, but it was unavoidable. Just at the boundary of Bayreuth her phone rang, and she answered it over her in-car system. It was Lotte.

"Hello Doris, where are you now? We've found Phil."

"I've just passed the sign for Meyernberg. And I can tell you that his last name is Großmann. I'm on the way – will you wait for me?"

"Of course. We've still got a few minutes up our sleeve. Till then."

A short time later the red BMW rolled into the station carpark, rather slower than last time, Doris always being more careful in bad weather. She parked, got out, and stepped right in the middle of a puddle that made her curse under her breath. Angry and still swearing at herself, she ran to the main entrance. Lotte was already waiting for her in the foyer with an escort of two uniformed officers. She introduced her companions – typical of Lotte, the pair of them apparently only had first names, Michel and Andy.

Then she explained, "I thought, if this Phil guy is really called Kill, you never know what you might be in for. So I thought it was important to have armed backup."

Doris nodded.

"As long as you haven't ordered up the tactical response unit," she murmured, making Lotte laugh.

"We could do that, couldn't we, Andy?"

Lotte winked at her colleagues as they quickly ran across the carpark to a patrol car.

"I don't like riding in the back, and these blue uniforms annoy me as well. I think we should have stuck with green."

Doris shook her head. Most German state police forces had switched from green to blue uniforms long ago, but conservative Bavaria had been reluctant to change.

"Only because you people in Bavaria are so stuck in your ways that you've only just changed over to blue."

"Franconia!" interjected Lotte indignantly, "and green was quite okay." Lotte considered Franconia as quite separate from Bavaria, even though most of Franconia had been incorporated into Bavaria over two centuries ago during the Napoleonic Wars.

"But blue is more convenient," Michel, the driver, put in.

"It doesn't matter. So, here's where we're at. This Phil has finally activated the USB memory stick, so that we've located him on Red Hill, and after you let me know, when you rang, that his name is Großmann, I could find the address easily. He actually lives on Red Hill, in Wacholderweg. That agrees with our tracking, so that's where we're going now. No flashing lights or siren, Michel."

"Goes without saying. I wouldn't have used them even if you hadn't told me."

They drove through the rain drenched town and Doris confirmed to herself that she had never been in this neck of the woods before. Of course, she knew where the large hospital complex of the Klinikum was, and she had once driven in the direction of Kulmbach, but she did not know this dormitory suburb that lay in-between. The Wacholderweg was a ring road above the hotel and beer garden of the Gaststätte Moosing. Phil Großmann's house number was easy to find. Michel turned off the motor and lights and the two women got out. They had agreed that Michel and Andi should wait in the car and would only intervene if the suspect started behaving aggressively.

There was a light on in the house, obscured by curtains. Outside motion sensors set off LED spotlights as Doris and Lotte approached the front door. They did not have to wait long after ringing for the man of the house to personally open up. The striking Elvis quiff flapped over his forehead while the rest of his blonde hair was tied back in a ponytail. Only the striking beard, that Lotte had called a 'Taliban beard', had in the meantime been transformed into an artwork of shaved skin and elaborate whiskers, obviously the latest fashion.

"Herr Großmann? Detective Chief Inspector Lech of the Bayreuth Criminal Investigation Department. We would like to ask you a few questions about your relationship with Tina Hermann. Can we come in?"

He did not look particularly surprised, and the feeling crept up on Doris that Albert Zweistein had already alerted him. After a perfunctory nod, he turned around and went ahead into a spacious room furnished in spartan fashion with chrome and leather. He pointed to a couch with a back that seemed to hover in the air.

"Please."

Phil himself took his place in a black leather armchair reminiscent of Captain Kirk's command post on the Starship Enterprise.

"Poor Tina. I read about it in the Courier. Well, she was often bitchy, but in truth she didn't deserve that," he declared rather feebly.

Lotte stared at him infuriated.

"Nobody deserves that."

"Might be, but despite that, murders happen day after day after day all over the world," he answered, without a change of expression.

Doris decided to put an end to the banter.

"Herr Großmann, apparently you were a good friend of Tina. Would you tell us when you got to know her and how intense your contact with her was?"

"A tea? I have an excellent pu-erh from Yunnan here, 67 years old. Unusual taste but altogether worth recommending. I would easily sacrifice two cups for the two of you."

"Thanks, no. Considering the cost of a tea that has been stored for so long, it could easily look like an attempt at bribery, and we all want to avoid that, don't we?"

Phil laughed.

"In fact, I don't suppose the two of you could afford such a treat. But, whatever, a missed opportunity. You can both have a swig of tap water any time you like if that is more non-committal. Let's get back to the reason for your visit. I got to know Tina in the spring, and since then we've had a loose relationship. She wasn't a simple person, you know? I could offer her so much but somehow or other I always had the feeling it annoyed her. She never managed to accept what our relationship offered her. She rather gave the impression that she was always ready to take off."

Doris raised an eyebrow and out of the blue shot in, "Tina worked for you as a prostitute."

Phil was not about to let himself be trapped.

"Definitely not. She was, however, a bit loose, like a bird that flits from tree to tree. I'm active in the fashion industry and know a whole bunch of interesting people all across Europe. So it wasn't that unusual that I brought Tina along to this or that event and made her acquainted with the rich and famous. It was her choice to make use of her quite personal advantages. These old guys are always looking for young blood, if you understand what I mean. So, in that way she had a good sideline going that didn't really disturb me. We had an open relationship. She wasn't worried if I spent a night with one of my models, either. But I never arranged anything. And I'll say it again that I never sent her out as a prostitute. Any more questions?"

Doris had not expected he would admit anything.

"Yes, if you in fact acquainted Tina with these men – as you put it – then you can certainly give us some names?"

"I could if I knew who she had been with. But since, however, I don't, I'm not going to place anyone under suspicion. Since Tina always made sure everything was above board, she would certainly have kept records for her tax return. Perhaps you'll have luck there."

The hint of an arrogant grin briefly played around the corner of his mouth before quickly disappearing.

"Herr Großmann, we found a note in Tina's purse."

This time Doris felt, just for a moment, that he went paler, but he quickly recovered himself.

"Aha, what sort of note?"

Doris threw it back at him.

"What do you think?"

"No idea. I've got enough money of my own without having to rummage around in Tina's purse."

He simply wouldn't let himself be caught out.

"'Only one year!' was written on the note. Can you imagine what that means?"

This time Phil did not hold her gaze.

"No, I can't. Perhaps she meant her work experience with this lawyer. Or she wanted to move out of home? No idea. Does anyone understand women?"

The chief inspector's tone became sharper.

"Perhaps it also meant that for some reason or other Tina was going to have to work for you for a year? How did you actually get to know the girl?"

Phil sighed and grimaced theatrically.

"I'm happy to tell you as often as you like: she wasn't working for me as a prostitute, and she didn't work for me in any other way. Yes, she was a good-looking girl, and I would have liked to have had her as a model for the summer collection but, unfortunately, she was purely and simply too gawky to run around in high heels. She clomped about like some sort of clumsy peasant. Pity. And I got to know her at Rosi's just before the fire. Any other questions?"

"Yes. Why did you visit Tina's parents?"

"I knew that Tina had photos of the two of us on her computer and I wanted to have them as a memento."

"Not, perhaps, to check what else Tina had on her computer? Files, for example, on the Crystal Spa in Fichtelberg, the property your friend Albert Zweistein would like to build on?"

This time Phil genuinely went pale.

"Zweistein and I are only fleeting acquaintances. We know each other via Tina. I know absolutely nothing about his plans in Fichtelberg."

As if it was prearranged, Lotte's phone went off at that moment, news from Tabea.

"Boss."

She passed the phone to Doris, who nodded, pleased.

"How is it then that our colleague at the station has found your name in the files dealing with the Crystal Spa?"

Phil searched for words, stammering uncomfortably, "Because ... I ... did a marketing campaign for Steinhart once. That's all ..."

"And with that you didn't by any chance have anything to do with Zweistein? Give him information, perhaps? Give him tips?"

Doris' voice was sounding more cutting. But the man opposite her had already regained his composure.

"No, I've already told you, I only know the guy in passing via Tina."

"Was he also one of her clients?"

"How would I know that? I didn't keep records and I didn't send her there, for heaven's sake. Holy shit, spare me all this crap. Tina was my girlfriend. Can't you see how it's affecting me?"

Doris examined the man thoughtfully.

"No, not really," she answered and stood up, followed closely by Lotte.

48

The trip back was spent in silence, apart from Lotte letting Doris know she had been able to make an appointment with Katharina Wagner. She had arranged for them to speak to her on Friday morning.

"Good."

Nothing more could be elicited from Doris.

They parted from Michel and Andi and went into the office. In the meantime it had gone eight o'clock, but since there was still no thought of knocking off, after a moment's reflection they dialled the number of a pizza service. A little later Doris had a pizza speciale in front of her on the table while Lotte had decided on a spicy salami pizza. While eating, Doris suddenly remembered something and reached for her phone.

"Hello? It's Doris Lech. I have to cancel tonight, unfortunately … Yes, I'm still in the office … Me too … Of course, I'd love to … See you soon."

She noticed Lotte's curious look and smiled.

"Might I ask …?" the young women enquired.

"You may. It's nothing spectacular. Dr Kollrab invited me out for a glass of wine this evening."

Doris could not stop her face from colouring a bit, which, as a trained interrogator, did not escape Lotte's notice.

"So … Dr Kollrab. I wouldn't have thought he had it in him. I've always thought he's only interested in corpses," she joked.

"Well, apparently not. And that's enough gossip. We have work to do."

Doris opened her computer and opened her emails. The next thing that Lotte heard from her boss was a choking sound.

"Doris? Boss? Is everything okay?"

Doris coughed and coughed until she finally freed herself of the piece of pizza that had gone down the wrong way.

"Yes, I'm okay. Well, forensics have put Tina's room under the magnifying glass today and have found something important."

"What then?" Lotte wanted to know.

"You won't like it, Lotte. In an envelope that Tina had pinned under her desk drawer were hidden several love letters. And they weren't written to Phil but to Albert."

Lotte swallowed.

"And? Have they found letters in the other direction, from Albert to Tina? No? Well, what is that really telling us? Tina was in a relationship with Phil and for some reason that we still don't know, she didn't leave him. At the same time she was secretly head over heels in love with Albert. I wouldn't blame her for that.

"I still can't imagine that Bertie is mixed up in this. You were there today, you saw him. He wouldn't hurt a fly. I'm sure he wasn't lying. He didn't have anything going on with Tina. And he is genuinely interested in me."

"Lotte, I really hope, from the bottom of my heart, that you're right, but as long as he is on the list of suspects, you should try to react more critically and be more neutral."

Lotte suppressed a yawn.

"Sorry, boss, but I've been here since six this morning and I can't keep my eyes open. Do we want to continue on tonight and then tomorrow morning have to recheck everything that we mess up now because we're so tired and unfocused, or would we be better off going home right away and starting afresh at six o'clock tomorrow morning?"

"Let me consider for a moment, Lotte – do we have anything to do that can't be put off, anything that under no circumstances can't wait till morning? Really nothing? Let me see, all suspects have been interviewed and the findings from Tina's room will still be here in the morning. Okay, agreed. That really is enough for today. Good night."

49

When Doris walked into the office next morning – by her lights extremely early, shortly after six – Lotte was already standing in the middle of the room writing eagerly on a whiteboard. The chief inspector stopped at the door, completely perplexed.

"Lotte, for heaven's sake. What's going on?"

Her assistant swept around and beamed at her.

"Good morning. We can detonate the bomb!"

"Well, some of the greetings in the last few days have really been pretty threatening: darts, antique shotguns. But now even a bomb? That's new, that's good, especially since this time it's us with the weapon. So, what is this all about, Lotte?"

Lotte seesawed from her heels to the balls of her feet and back again. It was noticeable that she had slept well and was totally ready for action.

"I spoke to my great-aunts."

"Ah, did they open their big book of fairy tales and, while the spinning wheel rattled away, read you stories from the murky past?" Doris said mockingly, but her malice splashed off Lotte like raindrops off a freshly washed car.

"No, not really. They were actually doing an internet search on elitepartner.de to find a husband for a niece of Aunt Greta," Lotte replied, grinning.

"What? Not for themselves? How self-sacrificing."

"Rubbish. Of course they look for themselves, but there's nothing reasonable on the market at their age. But now, do we want to solve a murder or gossip about dating sites?"

Doris took off her jacket, threw it over the back of her chair and sat down.

"Yeah, yeah, Okay. So, what did your aunts have to report?"

"They told me some things about the elder Zweistein and about the whole race of Zweisteins. I've just begun to write up all the important points here, a reconstruction of the rumour about the Zweistein Sonata."

Doris nodded appreciatively.

"And so early in the day. Congratulations. How many cups of coffee have you had already, I mean, to be functioning so well?"

Lotte laughed, "Caught out. Two cups at home and the pot is already empty here. I'll make some more."

While Lotte was busy with the coffee machine, Doris studied the notes on the whiteboard.

"What do all these different colours mean?" she wanted to know.

Lotte turned the coffee machine on, put the coffee container back in the cupboard and then came over.

"Right, this is how it works. Everything that we're certain about I've written in black. And the red, that's for the reports from witnesses and suspects. Speculation is in blue."

Again, Doris admired Lotte's work.

"This is really good. Okay, fire away."

"Let's start with the gossip about the elder Zweistein, that is to say, Herbert, the father of the composer. According to the diary of the woman who ran Blackthorn Mill, Anneliese Schlehmüller, her husband had to teach piano to Albert, the composer and son of Herbert Zweistein, and to his sister, Lisette. She wrote of a great injustice, because her husband was sent to the war, and of her frightful time as a widow. She was at that time subjected to weekly visits for sex from

Herbert Zweistein and wrote of a debt that had to be paid in this way. But what sort of debt? That she never wrote about."

"And why was it a great injustice, sending her husband to the war? Wasn't that usual at the time?"

Lotte nodded.

"Yes, of course. But the family had already lost two sons in the war and the father was therefore needed in the mill. Further on in the diary, Anneliese Schlehmüller claimed that her daughter, Margarethe, would never have committed suicide on account of not being able to get over the death of her father. She had, of course, been grief-stricken about losing him, and about the brothers who had died in action, but at the time she was overjoyed to be part of the play being put on for the school jubilee. She had been chosen to play the musical accompaniment. One day she didn't come home after the rehearsal, but – as we know – was found dead in front of the Girls' High School near the clock tower.

That's as much as we know about Margarethe. The trail goes cold there. All rather puzzling. Let's get to the rest of the Zweistein family. We know that Herbert was a rather irascible person, that he had the two children, that he acted like a lord of the manor in the worst sense of the term and forced Anneliese Schlehmüller to do him sexual favours to discharge an unnamed debt. His daughter, Lisette, was in the same year as Margarethe Schlehmüller at the Girls' High School. The son, Albert, wrote the famous Zweistein Sonata, which the aunts from Emtmannsberg are totally convinced actually flowed out of the quill of Siegfried Wagner. In any case, Albert only published this one piece. Something that strikes you in the published piece is the rather plodding opening compared with the rest of the sonata. Relevant to this is the audio file on Tina's computer, which I have written in blue, because it raises the very strong suspicion it could be a recording with the legitimate beginning of the sonata.

Unfortunately, we don't have any proof of that. Back to Albert. He died young of consumption in 1922. According to my aunts, in those days that was the common diagnosis for every kind of unidentified disease, but above all for those that you – I'm imitating Danda Bawedd here – only talk about in hushed tones."

This last comment was in dialect, in faithful imitation of 'Danda Bawedd'. Speaking in dialect annoyed Doris, even though in this case she worked out what 'Danda Bawedd' had said, and that 'Danda' meant 'aunt'. But 'Bawedd' was a complete mystery.

"Lotte, what is your aunt's name?" she enquired.

"Well, Danda Bawedd."

Expectant silence followed on both sides. Eventually, Doris gave in.

"Okay – the same game as with Ringsdorf. How do you spell your aunt's name?"

Now it was Lotte who was annoyed.

"Well B-A-B-E-T-T-E, how else?"

"Franconia," mumbled Doris, resigned, and received an equally incomprehensible dialectical version of 'Fishhead' in response.

"Lotte, I'm from Cologne. We aren't ..." protested Doris, failing to see how a derogatory name for Germans from the North and Baltic Sea coasts could apply to her, someone from Cologne on the Rhine River in the west of Germany over 350 kilometres from the nearest coast.

Lotte cut her off.

"No matter. We want to solve the murder, don't we? Right, let's proceed. Lisette married a distant cousin, who was also called Zweistein. Years later, he used the straightened circumstances of a certain family named Weigelt to buy a property off them neighbouring the Zweistein estate at Wolfsbach for a song, and, indeed, he used the money they had earned from the piano piece to help buy it. As Albert's sister, Lisette had inherited the rights to the sonata, because Albert had had no children. And their son, Karl Zweistein, topped it all off by selling the rights to the Zweistein Sonata to Hollywood, where it became the basis for the film music to a blockbuster movie."

Doris nodded thoughtfully, and added, "Yes, and the Weigelt family has tried to get their land back or, at the very least, secure compensation from Zweistein. Dr Held indicated that to you, didn't he? Okay – what we know about Tina: she was studying law and living a double life; she was apparently a high-class call girl; connected with her studies she had done work experience with Dr Held and worked there regularly in the semester breaks; and, because all good things come in threes, she also had a job in a dry cleaner's. That's why her sister, Anna, got her to dry clean the old costumes. A scrap of paper was found on her body with the word 'For' written in old-fashioned handwriting. According to Dr Held, she was following the story of the estate at Wolfsbach with great interest. That seems to be it for connections with the Zweisteins."

Lotte smiled sadly.

"Unfortunately, not completely. Tina was, at the least, well acquainted with the current Albert Zweistein, even if I don't like it. Nevertheless, I think it's unlikely that he, Dr Zweistein, is mixed up in the murder. What would he get out of it?"

"We'll get to the motives later. Before that we'll finish with the connections we've found to Tina. Tina had helped her friend, Marie-Claire, with the observation and cataloguing of rare species of plants and animals in the meadows round about the Wolfsbach estate. They had the common goal of establishing a nature reserve. No doubt Tina handled the correspondence with the responsible authorities. All of a sudden, however, she made a U-turn and declared that the whole area was being rezoned for housing. She categorically refused to introduce Marie-Claire to Zweistein, which led to a rift between the two girls. Tina wasn't just well acquainted with Albert, but had, besides that, a relationship with Phil Großmann. We suspect that she was working as a prostitute for him, that is to say, she was being forced to work as a prostitute for him. But we don't have any proof of that. So, is that everything?"

Lotte wrinkled her nose.

"I can't think of anything else. Should we get to the suspects and their motives?"

"Yes, we should. Let's start with my personal favourite, Phil. And my suspicion is the following – Phil got to know the girl, then, in ways that are still unknown, got her to work for him as a prostitute. There's an extremely high chance that she didn't do it of her own free will.

Now, some wild speculation about the note. She was under an obligation to him for a year but then something happened that made this time limit null and void. Perhaps she threatened to expose him as a pimp. Perhaps she found something in the files that made it possible to blackmail him."

Lotte uncapped the blue marker and wrote the name Phil in big letters on the whiteboard.

"Then her friend, Marie-Claire. In her case, we're not only dealing with someone who keeps poison arrow frogs illegally, but also with someone who threatened me with a shotgun, which all points to a certain propensity for violence, and we're also dealing with someone who knows how to use a blowpipe and tranquilliser arrows. So, she has the capacity to commit a murder like this. And the motive? She was betrayed by her best friend and left in the lurch for what she sees as a vile building project. And that's not all, no – Tina refusing to introduce Marie-Claire to her friend, Albert, left Marie-Claire with no chance of presenting her case."

Marie-Claire's name was written on the whiteboard.

"Then, as much as I'm sorry to say it, Albert Zweistein. Let's assume that the wild story about the Zweistein Sonata is true, and let's assume that Tina found proof of it, then perhaps she was blackmailing Albert. There was a lot at stake for him if this were the case. In the worst-case scenario, he would have to transfer all the money that the sonata had ever earned to the Wagner family. And even if the profits are not, or are only partly, in dispute, then, nevertheless, there still remains the possibility of compensation for pain and suffering. The outstanding example of this is the former defence minister, zu Guttenberg, who was exposed for plagiarism of his doctoral thesis and forced to pay €20,000 to charity in compensation. In any case, and this speaks against this theory, Albert died in 1922 but Siegried Wagner not until 1930. That means he was still alive when the piece was published. Why didn't he say something if he had actually composed the sonata? Or had he in fact consented to the fraud? Did Albert possibly pay him so the piece could be published under his name? So many unanswered questions, but, nevertheless, we have to write Albert Zweistein on the whiteboard."

Lotte gave Doris an indignant look, but it got her nowhere. So, she wrote Zweistein's name as small as possible in the bottom righthand corner.

"Anyone else? For the record, Dr Held, the darts champion. We can only speculate about possible motives. Did he possibly discover Tina's double life? Was he in the end a customer of his work experience student? It wouldn't be the first time … or did she discover something in his files that she could blackmail him with? I wouldn't personally consider him a suspect, but we do need to write him up for the sake of completeness."

"And the same goes for his secretary. The woman isn't completely squeaky clean. She has an unbridled hatred of

Tina, and even accused her of trying to poison her. Someone who believes things like that is capable of a lot. And who's to say that it's only Dr Held who uses his dartboard for practice?”

Responding to her boss's nod, Lotte wrote both names on the whiteboard.

“There's still the Green Hill, the Wagner clan. Lotte, I thought about it a lot last night but actually I can't imagine why they would be involved. Nevertheless, tomorrow I'll ask Katharina Wagner what she knows about the Zweistein Sonata and what legal implications she would envisage if there was something in the plagiarism allegations.”

Lotte threw her head back sulkily but still produced the blue marker and wrote up the name Wagner, albeit in even smaller letters than she had written Albert Zweistein.

Lotte took a deep breath and put the marker down.

“And what now?” she asked.

Doris suppressed a smile.

“What would you suggest?” she asked the younger woman, encouraging her to take the initiative.

Lotte did not need to think about it for long.

“I would propose a search of Phil's place,” she declared with enthusiasm.

“Ditto. So, let's get going. We'll need to get a search warrant.”

50

The mobile phone had lain for a good while on the heater, packed in rice. The time had now finally arrived to risk it and try to bring it back to life. Why of all things had it dropped into the fountain when Tina fell down dead. Still, with a bit of luck it would now give up its secrets.

Carefully put in the plug, carefully turn the phone on. How stupid some people were, not to put in a password.

Aaah, there it is. Very good. Just a minute, have a quick look – here is the message to me. That must be the last message she sent.

Wait a minute. What's this? The slut sent the photo to someone else!?!

By WhatsApp to a Sara3. Who the hell was that?

Nice profile picture. Fabulous, the strawberry blonde hair. Okay, Ginger, I'll give you a call. I'll find you; you can rely on that. But now to get rid of the phone. How stupid it would be, if the police got me ...

51

When the police turned up the owner of the house was away on business. Only a housekeeper, completely beside herself and intermittently ringing her boss, ran screaming after the officers. Phil was raging so loudly that Doris could hear him without the phone being on speaker mode. In fact, he yelled so loudly at his Colombian au pair that everyone present could easily hear every word – as long as they knew enough German, which could not be said for Conchita. The South American beauty had by far the biggest and darkest eyes in the room, but, unfortunately, no grasp of the situation. And Phil was away in Munich. It would not matter how hard he thrashed his BMW Z4 roadster, he would still arrive too late. That was as clear to him as it was to the police officers, who were quite relaxedly packing away file after file, as well as all electronic devices, and who were meticulously searching drawers for documents and photos. Only Conchita lacked the imagination to realise how much time it would take to drive the stretch from Munich to Bayreuth if you were not Captain Kirk and could not have yourself beamed up. She was sobbing into her phone.

"Jefe, Jefe, please, quickquick, come. La policía está aquí! Ven rápido a casa! I much scared! Tengo mucho miedo. Quickquick, come."

When Lotte tried to calm the girl down, she only managed the opposite. When she lightly touched her arm, Conchita screamed and cried even louder, firmly convinced to have been mistaken for the boss of a drug cartel.

"We're getting nowhere here," Lotte complained, whose school Spanish had long been forgotten. "Does anyone here speak Spanish? Otherwise, we're going to need to get a translator before the girl drives us completely round the bend."

No one there could speak Spanish, so Lotte called the station and explained what was going on. She was assured a translator would be requested but was informed that, going by experience, it could take a while.

"Tranquilo," she said, trying to make a connection, and pushed the au pair into a chair. Eventually, the girl noticed that it all apparently had nothing to do with her and that she personally was out of the firing line, a realisation that in fact did manage to calm her down a bit.

Almost all the items had already been packed up and stowed away in the VW van when a translator finally arrived. Doris explained to him what he should say to Conchita to explain the facts to her.

Then she had another idea.

"Please tell her, in case she is scared that her boss will be furious at her, that she can come with us to the station – he'll show up there anyway. It would be a miracle if he didn't."

Conchita listened to the tirade of Spanish and nodded violently, tears streaming down her cheeks.

"Muchas gracias."

"Oh, yes. A last thing. Can you ask her what exactly she does here for a living?"

"Housekeeper."

Doris's brow furrowed.

"If I am under the impression … ask her if she is working for Phil as a prostitute."

Doris was buffeted by a tirade of indignant Spanish, which, undeterred, she let bounce off her.

"Tell her that she doesn't need to worry about admitting it. She isn't the only one. And her fellow worker was murdered."

Conchita just about fell over herself with her increasingly rapid explanations, again broke down in tears and finally put her face in her hands.

"And?" Doris wanted to know.

"Yes."

"So many words for something that was obvious, anyway. I would like her to be interrogated more closely at the station. And I want to know if she wants to bring charges."

Two hours later, Conchita had made her statement and after some convincing, also brought charges. Her greatest fear was being immediately sent back to Colombia, but on that count Doris could reassure her.

"Don't worry, we don't deport victims of a punishable crime. I'm sure we can find you a new place of work, this time with a nice and respectable boss."

Lotte interrupted.

"Or she can come with me to Emtmannsberg? Our neighbour would be thankful if she had a housekeeper. She has bad rheumatism and can no longer do everything that she wants to."

"Lotte, why am I not surprised? Here everyone knows someone who can help someone else, or am I wrong?"

Lotte beamed.

"You've finally worked it out, boss. You'll see, you'll settle in here and become a dyed-in-the-wool Upper Franconian yet."

"God preserve me. First let's solve our case. What have we sorted through so far?"

"Three of the four boxes from Phil's place. And as for the fourth, we're on to it. Tabea grabbed the computer but is struggling with the password."

She went back to the box, which was lying on the floor in front of her desk and rummaged around in it.

Suddenly she called out, "Ha, I've got something here," and dragged out a brown C4 envelope. She triumphantly let the contents slide onto her boss's desk, who in turn gazed dumbfounded at the photos that spilt out. They showed Tina and Phil involved in an unmistakable activity.

"Well, how about that. Perhaps he used these to blackmail her, to make her toe the line? And what else do we have here?"

She leafed through some printed sheets and her gaze was held by one signature that stood out on two pages.

"Look, Tina Hermann. What has she signed there? A contract that definitely contravenes public morality laws – she commits herself to work for him for a year and to visit the men whose addresses he gives her. She has to appear in designer label clothes and to do whatever they expect of her. The customers' wishes are to be fulfilled without protest. So that's why the note, 'Only one year'. That explains a lot. And the second contract concerns a credit with the sort of extortionate interest that means it can just about never be repaid … and with a clause that her work contract is automatically extended until it is. So, irredeemable for ever and a day. The poor thing – how did he get her to sign it?"

The answer to that was supplied by Tabea, who came in a bit later.

"We haven't managed to crack the computer yet. This guy sure is cunning. But we've discovered something else that should interest you. Look, Love Beer is written on this small bottle, and guess what's in it – knockout drops. A small amount will make the victim talkative, a stronger dose causes a complete blackout, makes someone unable to resist whatever is suggested to them."

Doris got excited.

"Doing things like sign insane contracts?"

"That and the rest," Tabea confirmed.

The next moment the door was almost torn from its hinges, so violently did Phil rip it open.

"Have you all gone completely mad?" he roared, his face flushed in fury.

Tabea inconspicuously shut the door behind him.

"Herr Großmann. Good of you to come to us – you've spared us going in search of you. I'm arresting you on suspicion of procuring women for prostitution under Article 181a, Paragraph 1, Number 2 of the criminal code. And I'm optimistic that we'll be able to add a charge of murder to that."

"What? Tell me, what have you been taking? Is it still having an effect?"

Doris laughed coldly.

"It's not your love beer, anyway. Just give in, Herr Großmann. We've found the photos of you and Tina …"

"… they're private photos and they're not against the law. Give them to me."

"They're prima facie evidence. Besides that, we have a so-called employment contract, which contravenes public morality laws, along with a usurious credit contract. You used these contracts to chain Tina to you and the poor girl was presumably so shamed by them that she couldn't confide in anyone or go to the police. And now I would like to know everything you can think of about Tina Hermann. And make it snappy."

Phil Großmann still did not crack.

"I don't admit anything – we only wrote those contracts for fun when the two of us had had too much to drink. That they're not legally binding is clear to anyone – and Tina was a law student. Who would have known that better than her? Sometimes our sense of humour was a bit offbeat, and that's an example."

He furiously smashed his right fist on the table, but it was equally not that easy to make Doris lose her composure.

"Okay, have it your own way. Does the name Conchita Vina mean anything to you?"

The chief inspector fixed her gaze on him, but Phil did not lower his eyes.

"Of course the name means something to me. Do you take me for a fool? That is the name of the Colombian au pair who works as my housekeeper. You met her yourself when you turned up with your search warrant. What's that got to do with anything?"

Doris lent back and reached for a thin file. She took a thin handwritten page out of it.

"Do you know what I have here? Presumably not, so I'll tell you. The signed statement of your au pair. According to this, she was forced by you to meet other men and to go to bed with them. There is a formal charge against you accompanying it. Are you going to persist in telling me that Tina's contracts were just a joke?"

Phil raised his eyebrows.

"Prove the opposite. And this Conchita only wants to get back at me because she wanted three days a week off and I'd only give her two. You can't do anything to me."

"But I can. And I will. These contracts signed by you and Tina alone are enough, because a court won't see them as examples of humour, but as contracts that contravene public morality laws that were designed to subject Tina to your will. And once we have exhausted that topic, then I'd like to know exactly why you murdered Tina."

"For God's sake, that again – I didn't kill her. I'd be careful if I were you. It's true. I did coerce her and blackmail her. I threatened to tell her parents what she had done when she was high on the love beer. But that was all. She was a decent girl."

"And that decent girl discovered something in Dr Held's files that she could blackmail you with. What was it? Was it in the file labelled Crystal Spa? Or was it something in the file labelled Eierberg? Herr Großmann, we'll find out, I guarantee you that. And if you confess, that will end up going in your favour."

Furious, Phil jumped up.

"I'm not going to confess to anything, because there isn't anything to confess to," he roared, his voice cracking at the last words. He gasped for air before he continued screaming.

"Damn it, I don't have anything on my conscience. Why would I have killed the best horse in my stable? Go on, search, burrow through the files from front to back and back again. I promise you, you won't find anything because there's nothing there. She wasn't blackmailing me. What the hell."

Doris struggled to keep a calm expression on her face, although she was boiling over inside.

Finally, she pressed the bell under her desk and, when a uniformed colleague came in, just said, "You have the right to call your lawyer. Take him away."

While Phil Großmann was being led to a cell, Doris attempted to smile weakly at Lotte and Tabea.

"I've always wanted to say that."

52

"And now?"

Lotte was sitting at her desk, a coffee mug next to her.

"Do you believe him or not?"

She looked expectantly at Doris.

"I don't know. On the one hand, it seems logical to me that Phil is the murderer – and not only because his Facebook name is 'Kill'. After all, he only confessed to the procuring when we said it straight to his face and produced the evidence at the same time. On the other hand, he has admitted the procuring but vehemently denied the murder. Of course, there's a big difference between being sentenced to five years jail and a life sentence. Despite that, I'm not sure. The circumstantial evidence goes against him, and our line of questioning is conclusive enough for a charge. But I would really like incontrovertible proof … for my own peace of mind, do you understand?"

"Tina's phone hasn't shown up at Phil's, has it? If only we had it, then that would be a big help. I also don't know if I think Phil is a murderer. Of all the suspects he is the most logical culprit, and I don't think Tina meant anything to him, but would he kill her if she was trying to blackmail him?"

Doris stared at the screensaver until her eyes hurt. She had a headache as well. She pulled the top shelf of her desk open and rummaged around for a packet of aspirin, which she waved about.

"I need one today. I have to be fighting fit again by this evening. It's the show at Richard Wagner Grammar School – of course, RWG – and Frau König, my landlady, has organised a ticket for me. Did your family go yesterday?"

Lotte sighed.

"No. Lisa would have liked to have seen us go yesterday. But first night tickets? They went quickly – the current and former teachers got to go, and there were a few VIPs as well. Lisa said Katharina Wagner was actually there. We're going tomorrow night. There's still another performance then. Lisa says that because of the big demand two more performances will be put on in Christmas week. Anyway, enjoy the night. What do you think? Do we knock off early today? We've got enough time off in lieu up our sleeves."

Lotte glanced quickly at her phone.

"Three thirty – we don't need to take time off in lieu, we've just finished a ten-hour shift. I'm going to go into town for a bit, go for a stroll, look for the first Christmas presents. See you tomorrow, then."

53

Lotte ambled across the Marktplatz, Bayreuth's old market square, nowadays incorporated into the inner-city pedestrian zone, and was happy that it wasn't raining. She poked around in this and that shop and ended up standing in front of the tax office to look at the construction of the rapidly growing Winter Village. It would open in ten days. After that, it would be overflowing every evening with people who were important, who thought they were important or who simply wanted to have fun.

Lotte already knew she would not come here much because she could not stand the cold. She liked having a good time, often and a lot, but only where it was warm. For the same reason she would never be so stupid as to hit it off with an ice hockey coach, like Julia Lehmann, Doris' predecessor, who had since taken parental leave. No matter.

She was just about to go on her way when she felt a hand on her arm.

"Well, I've come to Bayreuth a few days too early, have I, Lotte?"

Lotte knew the voice. She whirled round and gave her old school friend, Sara, a big hug.

"Wow, Sara, how great to see you. You're studying out of town, aren't you? In Regensburg? Music, if I'm not wrong? Are you here for the anniversary?"

Sara nodded excitedly.

"Yes, imagine – I'm here for five days, and we can meet up with everyone from school and relive the good old days again. It's only a pity that Rosi's has burned down."

"Yes, true. It's a real shame. But we'll soon find somewhere else where we can make ourselves comfortable. Have you already run into a lot of people?"

"No, unfortunately not. I've been trying all day to reach Tina. Tell me, you're with the police, aren't you – have you perhaps arrested her? If not, can you perhaps try to locate her phone. Is that possible?"

Lotte went pale.

"Oh God, Sara, you don't know, do you!?! Tina is dead. She was murdered a couple of days ago – found poisoned in the Dammwäldchen. It was a headline in the Courier, but, of course, you're not here anymore."

"What? Tina … dead?"

Sara stared at Lotte in disbelief.

"No, say it isn't true. It's not possible. And murdered? Who would do something like that? Have you caught whoever did it? Why would she be killed? Would she …? Oh my God, no. I didn't know, I only got here today, and I haven't read the Courier. There was something about a murdered student in the Regensburg paper, but I didn't for a moment think …"

Sara began to cry silently. At first single tears rolled over her cheeks, then, however, they flowed uncontrollably, and she sank onto Lotte's shoulder and bawled her eyes out.

Lotte steered her school friend to a bench not far away opposite a bratwurst booth.

"Come, sit down for a bit, Sara. Actually, the way it's looking we might have had success today – at least, we've arrested a suspect. It will soon be on the local radio news, so it's all right telling you. Did you still have a lot of contact with Tina?"

Sara rummaged in her handbag for a tissue, and Lotte automatically grabbed for her jacket pocket where there was a packet hidden.

"Thanks. We weren't really close anymore but now and again we rang or wrote to each other. It's just not possible. She sent me a photo just a day or so ago. It was strange though. This photo arrived of a page of sheet music and the message just said, 'Do you know what this is?' When I answered back, she didn't reply. Since then, I've tried to reach her a few times without success. I was annoyed that she first tried to make me curious and then left me in the lurch. And it was because she was dead ..."

Lotte pricked up her ears.

"Sara, show me the picture – it's possible it has something to do with the murder."

Sara got out her phone and started to look for it.

"Hopefully I haven't deleted it. This old thing doesn't have much memory. Ah, no. Here it is. Look here."

She held the screen under Lotte's nose and Lotte tapped on the picture, making it bigger, her eyes popping with excitement.

"Sara, we have to forward this to my boss immediately. This is the exact missing piece of the puzzle that we've been looking for. And look at the time it was sent – right before Tina's death. Perhaps she sent you a valuable clue to her murderer. May I ...?"

Sara nodded a bit confused, but Lotte, fingers flying, was already typing Doris Lech's number. She had hardly sent off the picture when she pulled out her own phone and tried to reach her boss. In vain. She only got voice mail.

"Damn it!"

Lotte put her phone back in her pocket.

"She's turned her phone off. Presumably because she wanted to go to the theatre today. What time is it? Already after half past six? Yes, she'll already be in RWG. The show begins at seven. Sara, what do you think of this music? You're studying music, what do you think it is?"

The young woman shook her head sadly.

"I've asked myself that as well. It looks to be pretty old. The first page of a piano piece. From the style I would say from the beginning of the twentieth century. It is reminiscent of the Zweistein Sonata, but it sounds more polished. And at the top – look, can you see that? There's something written at the top that I can hardly decipher. Who can still read old handwriting like this these days? I think it says, 'For my beloved A. from S.W. in everlasting remembrance'. Do you see? That's what it is, isn't it?"

"Yes – this is completely crazy. Do you know what? We've been looking for exactly this piece of paper. It's been like searching for a needle in a haystack, but without knowing exactly what we were looking for. Insane, don't you think? And Tina sent it to you. But … but it looks like it gets our suspect off the hook … at least, I think so … oh my goodness. Sara, I think I was right all along. We have to look at the Festival Theatre, at the Wagner family."

Sara shook her head, completely at a loss.

"I've got no idea what you're talking about, Lotte. Besides that, you must have Tina's phone. The photo has to be on it, too."

"No. That's just it, we don't have it. It's gone, disappeared. But perhaps we should simply check once again in the Dammwäldchen. Tabea has complained that the scene of the crime was cleared too quickly. Perhaps there was sloppy work, and the phone is in truth somewhere there in the shrubbery? Let's go, come on."

Lotte sprang up from the bench, grabbed Sara's hand and dragged her up with her.

"For God's sake, come on, Sara."

Off they went, past the life-size dinosaur in front of the Museum of the Prehistoric World, over the cobblestones next to the Town Church, past Wiesenmüller, the butcher, getting a hint of the aroma of meat loaf as they passed, through the Steingräber Passage next to the world famous piano makers, Steingräber and Sons, where, as is so often the case, melancholy music echoed off the walls and over the Dammallee, the embankment lane they needed to cross to get to the Dammwäldchen. Something else occurred to Lotte on the way.

"Sara, you've got to have played this music, haven't you? Do you still have the melody in your head?"

"Sure. It's my job to take notice of things like that."

The student hummed the melody, Lotte listening carefully. She wrinkled her nose and nodded.

"Yes, it's exactly as I thought. I know this melody. I've heard it before."

"Where then?" Sara wanted to know.

"Sara, I'm not allowed to tell you that yet. But I promise you, when it is all cleared up, then I'll tell you everything. Let's keep going. We have to look for this phone."

Sara looked around. Grey rainclouds were building up again and it would soon be dark. The modest bushes that were planted between the Linden trees in the Dammwäldchen swallowed a bit more of the light. The babbling fountain made a steady noise but, apart from the odd car passing by the park, nothing could be heard in the twilight. It was eerie, especially when you thought that a few days ago a murder had happened here. Sara hunched her shoulders, freezing.

"Lotte, leave it for now. It would be better to ring the station and get a few officers over with spotlights. How are we going to find anything here? We don't even have flashlights."

"We've got our phones. And what do you think they're going to say to me if I demand assistance? Forensics were here, you know. They would feel like I was treading on their toes if I questioned their work. Come on, turn on the light on your phone and look with me. Our phone lights will just have to do. You do have a light on your phone?"

"Sure, of course …" Sara answered hesitantly. She didn't want to admit that being there really gave her the creeps. "Where was Tina exactly …?"

Lotte made a movement with her phone, faintly lighting up the fountain.

"Here, next to the fountain. She was hit in the neck by a poison dart."

"What? But that means the murderer lay in wait … Lotte? That could happen to us right now, too. I'm scared."

Sara's hand trembled slightly and the trembling ray of light from her phone zigzagged on the ground.

"Nonsense. Why would the murderer be here now? He doesn't know we are here," Lotte replied resolutely.

"Because a murderer always returns to the scene of the crime? Because he's also looking for the phone? Lotte, I'm scared, really. Please let's go."

"No, you're being stupid. No normal person is afraid when they have police protection! Come on, help me look."

She enthusiastically lit up a bush. But when she turned round and saw the panic in Sara's face, she felt sorry for her and went up closer to her friend.

"Sara, please. It's really important."

At that moment Lotte's phone rang and Sara flinched.

"Don't answer it – it's certain to be the murderer, who's observing us," she whispered. But Lotte only laughed.

"Rubbish. It's a friend of mine. Just a moment, Sara."

Sara leant against the advertising pillar that stood in the middle of the little park. At least here nobody can jump me from behind, she thought, to reassure herself. That did not work. She strained to listen in the approaching darkness. Every small crackle and rustle made her flinch. And Lotte just went on talking to a friend, totally oblivious. Why wasn't Lotte afraid when she was totally beside herself?

Like a bolt out of the blue, a terrifying thought occurred to her that she was powerless to resist. What if Lotte was involved in it? If she was, she now knew that the only proof of the music was on her phone. And Lotte was the only one she had told about it. Fear and panic wrapped around her like an icy cloth. There would only be one solution from Lotte's point of view ... getting rid of Sara. And she was presumably at this very moment speaking to an accomplice about how they were going to do it.

Sara felt her heart beating with panic and heard nothing but the blood rushing in her ears. Lotte, who was standing only a few metres away, took her phone from her ear as if in slow motion and turned round to Sara. She would do it right now ... run, Sara! For heaven's sake, run!!!

Without considering it further Sara followed her instinct, turned on her heel and ran.

54

Lotte moved a few steps to the side. Sara must not hear who she was speaking to.

"Yes, hello Bertie. To what do I owe the honour?"

"Lotte, I'm sorry that everything has gone so badly between the two of us. You really are important to me, I would so much like to see you again."

"Bertie, that might be so, but as long as I'm stuck in the middle of the investigation, it's not a good idea."

Soft laughter came from the phone.

"Lotte, do you think I'm stupid? I heard the news on the radio. You've arrested the murderer. What's the problem, then?"

"We haven't got the murderer, we've just arrested a suspect. We live under the rule of law here and he hasn't been convicted yet."

"But where's the problem? Do you really believe that I have anything to do with the murder?"

"No …"

"So, we can meet for a beer, can't we? Completely straightforward, somewhere in town. Oskar's? In half an hour?"

"Oh no, Bertie, I really can't – okay, fine. Anyway, I'm already in town."

"Really? That works out great, I'm actually out and about right now, walking down Bismarckstraße towards town. Are you near me?"

"Yes, I'm with a friend in the Dammwäldchen. Is it okay to take her with us? A chaperone certainly isn't a bad idea, is it, considering how complicated everything is with the investigation?"

Albert took a moment to answer, just enough to let it show that he was not really enthusiastic about the suggestion.

"Okay, she can come, I suppose. It's probably not such a bad idea. Heh, are you still in the Dammwäldchen? I'm right by there. I'm standing at the traffic lights to the Ring."

"Good, till then. I'm looking forward to it."

Lotte slowly put her phone away. Her plan to look exhaustively for Tina's missing phone was dead. It had been a spur of the moment idea, anyway – the others would certainly have found it if it had been here. It was nothing but unconsidered overenthusiasm, nothing else. She turned around to Sara.

"Sara, I have just … Sara?"

Lotte looked at her friend in bewilderment as she suddenly took off as if pursued by the Furies, straight across the Dammwäldchen and towards RWG.

"Sara? Wait, why don't you? Sara!"

Lotte sprinted after the music student, who now began screaming in panic as she turned round and saw over her shoulder that Lotte was following her.

"Sara! What on earth's got into you? Sara!"

Sara wouldn't stop but ran on further in the direction of the intersection. Her strawberry blonde locks shone for a moment in the light of a streetlamp as she crossed over. A man approached her from Wittelsbacherring, paused for a moment when he saw her, and then came on even quicker – Lotte's accomplice!

Sara shrieked again loudly and hurriedly looked around. She was caught in a trap. There! A light was on in the auditorium of RWG. The side entrance was also bathed in a golden yellow beam of light. Sara darted sideways, pulled the heavy wooden door open and clattered up the few steps in the direction of the auditorium – and directly into the arms of a woman, who was obviously on the way to the toilet.

"Hey, stop! Not so fast, young lady. What is wrong? Can I help?"

The stranger held Sara softly but firmly by the shoulders, but at that moment the heavy outside door opened once more and Sara, overcome by panic, tried to tear herself away. Her pursuer ran in, stopped abruptly, and for what seemed like an eternity, Doris Lech and Albert Zweistein silently eyed each other over Sara's shoulders.

Then the spell broke and Doris, who steadfastly held on to Sara, spoke.

"So, we meet again, Dr Zweistein. Would you be so kind as to explain to me what all this means?"

He laughed bitterly.

"Do you really think it was all in vain? I don't admit defeat so quickly."

Zweistein felt in his jacket pocket and as quick as a flash pulled out a dart. Doris swore at herself for not having brought her service weapon with her. She protectively pressed Sara to her.

"What has this girl done to you? Leave her in peace. Whatever has happened – if you stop now, it will mitigate your penalty. Be sensible, give yourself up."

Again, he laughed, hard and bitter.

"Mitigating? Don't make me laugh. Scot-free is the magic word. Lady Inspector, you know too much, and this girl as well. I'm sorry for both of you."

"Zweistein, are you mad. Do you know how many people are in the auditorium watching the performance?"

"Ha, you just said it, in the auditorium – it's not going to be of much use to you. Because you …"

Doris pulled Sara aside, let herself fall, heard Sara's shrill cry, and saw as she fell that Zweistein was also heading for the floor. The investigator rolled off to the side, got back on her feet and hurried to help her assistant, who had come up behind Zweistein and without hesitating had rudely transported him into the world of dreams with a well-aimed karate punch. It was quickly established that Zweistein was in fact unconscious.

"Good work, Lotte!" she praised her young colleague, who looked sadly at the doctor lying on the floor.

"You were right, Doris. Oh my God, I was so stupid."

A tear formed in the corner of Lotte's eye and, embarrassed, was wiped away with a sleeve. Lotte looked around at Sara and ran over to help her friend.

"Sara, are you okay? Is everything all right?"

Sara stared at her anxiously but then realised that Lotte actually was one of the good guys and silently embraced her.

"Lotte, do you by any chance have some handcuffs on you?" Doris wanted to know, but her colleague indicated that she did not.

By now a gaggle of people had streamed out of the auditorium, alerted by Sara's cry. The spectators talked excitedly with one another, and a couple of actors came running in as well. Lotte recognised her sister, Lisa, who had hitched up her heavy woollen skirt to stumble up the stairs.

"Lisa, quickly fetch Frau Grimm. And she should look to see if she has some handcuffs among her props, at least ones that lock properly."

She then made an emergency call to get backup.

Just a little later the probable murderer of Tina Hermann was led away – in genuine handcuffs.

With a sigh of relief Doris took a look around. She noticed a blonde woman who was looking at her thoughtfully. After a moment of reflection, she recognised her as Katharina Wagner. She went up to her and introduced herself.

"I thought you went to yesterday's performance?" she then asked.

Katharina Wagner nodded.

"Yes, but I was free tonight and I enjoyed it very much yesterday, so I wanted to come back again today. Do you know, I was a student here once. Like your colleague, Lotte Kerner. She told me that on the phone. Unfortunately, I can't remember her, she was probably after my time."

"Quite astonishing – in Bayreuth everybody knows everybody else, don't they?" said Lotte with a smile.

"Indeed. Frau Kerner and I are obviously the shameful exceptions. You have made an appointment for tomorrow – can we perhaps conduct it here straight away? Then you'll save yourself a trip. Or is that rather inconvenient?"

Doris dismissed the suggestion with a short glance at the wooden door that had just slammed behind Dr Albert Zweistein.

"I think it's all sorted itself out. We can happily cancel the appointment. It's been a pleasure to get to know you."

Doris went slowly over to Frau Grimm. Her right ankle throbbed a bit, because she had unluckily landed on the step as she fell, but it was bearable.

"Frau Grimm, what do you think? Do you want to go on with the performance? I would like it very much. And if you could organise two places for Lotte and Sara, the evening would be perfect."

55

It was late morning, and it was like a railway station in Doris Lech's office. Eventually, the inspector came to a firm decision.

"So, before we have to close up here because of over-crowding, let's adjourn the briefing to the meeting room three doors down. At least there we'll be able to talk about the case in peace."

She went out and droves of colleagues followed her. Lotte was naturally one of them, as were Tabea and Franziska, Michel and Andi, and even the public prosecutor, Strasser, who had insisted on visiting her.

"I wanted you to know that I deliberately held back from interfering in your first case," Strasser rasped out the moment he laid eyes on Doris. "People like to accuse me of putting colleagues under too much pressure and being too temperamental. Your predecessor certainly liked arguing with me. But I didn't want you to feel hurried when you were just starting out. And you have solved this case, with the help of your colleague, Kerner, in a really professional way. Two arrests right away. Commendable, commendable. Unfortunately, I have to let you know that your honeymoon period officially ends as of this moment. All the best for our time working together."

A dumbfounded Doris shook the proffered hand and stared after Strasser as, with a spring in his step, he headed in the direction of the lift.

"Oh, oh, apparently you're in Bonsai's good books," whispered Lotte and winked at her.

"Bonsai?"

"Well, just look at him – the man's built like a tree, so he's called Bonsai. The whole station calls him that. His temper tantrums are feared. His own work is first-class, so he expects the same from everybody else, preferably yesterday rather than today. But today he is quite amiable. Let's hope it stays that way for a long time. "

They sat themselves down at the large meeting room conference table. Doris was wanting to get straight down to her comments on the case when there was a short knock at the door. Dr Rainer Kollrab stuck his head in.

"May I?" he asked.

"Naturally, sit down by all means. So, what do you all still want to know about the murder of Tina Hermann?"

Tabea was the first to speak.

"It's still not clear to me what Zweistein had to do with Tina Hermann. I thought they barely knew each other."

"Well, the good doctor was feeding us a line. He actually met Tina in the spring. After a couple of weeks, he and Phil mixed up their love beer drops for her, had a wild orgy with her and made a nice film of it to blackmail her with. It seems Zweistein was somehow in debt to his friend. How, we still don't know. Tina wanted out but felt she couldn't do so legally. So, she looked for something that she could use to blackmail Phil or Albert. When she went to dry-clean the costumes, she found the page of sheet music with the dedication in a pocket of one of the dresses. Now, Dr Held had told her of the rumour about the Zweistein Sonata, so she realised that the dedication was her ticket to freedom. She called Zweistein, who as a doctor knows a lot about poisons. It must have been one of his hobbies and it seems he had ordered the frog poison cocktail a while ago, allegedly to analyse its composition and mode of operation more closely. To use it to get Tina out of the way was obvious. She summoned him to the Dammwäldchen in broad daylight, probably because she felt safer there, but he ambushed her, threw his poison dart, and fished the phone out of the water in the fountain. And it so happened that he had got the phone to work again on the very evening that Lotte and Sara were out together. When he saw the girl coming towards him, he recognised her from her WhatsApp profile picture and ran after her – into our arms. If Lotte hadn't been there who knows how it would have ended up."

Lotte blushed.

"Not worth mentioning. I just did my job."

"Yes, and very well, at that, Lotte. Any other questions?"

Rainer Kollrab wanted to know what would happen if the real composer of the Zweistein Sonata was made public.

"We really don't know. On the one hand, the Zweisteins would naturally be in the centre of an enormous scandal. But since Albert Senior is long since dead, it would probably be no more than a storm in teacup, something they could safely sit out. It's also hard to say what the financial consequences would be. From a legal perspective all claims made after seventy years would be null and void, and our sonata is around a hundred years old. Of course, you could speculate if this time limit still applies when stolen intellectual property, so to speak, is illegally published. And what of the royalties from the Hollywood blockbuster? Would the time limit still apply to them as well, since the original sonata was altered for the film? All this, however, is a matter for lawyers specialising in copyright law to figure out. Whether, and to what extent, the Wagner family could proceed against the Zweisteins, I can't judge. In any case, Siegfried Wagner gave Zweistein the sonata as a present. And it is also not completely insignificant that he didn't protest about the publication of the sonata under Zweistein's name. That speaks for it not having happened against Siegfried's wishes."

"But why was the page of sheet music in the costume pocket in the first place?" Tabea asked. "It's an absolute puzzle to me."

Lotte raised her head.

"May I, boss? We don't know everything – some is pure speculation. But what we do know for sure is what we have discovered from some diaries of the old Zweistein, that is, the first Albert, while searching the Zweistein manor house. In his diaries we found out that Margarethe Schlehmüller, who fell from the clocktower a hundred years ago, under no circumstances committed suicide. We can piece together what actually happened. Margarethe's father had apparently stolen the music from the manor house. Perhaps he wanted to blackmail Zweistein, it is not completely clear. In any case, the father of the first Albert used his connections to have Schlehmüller sent to the front. The music, however, remained lost until Albert by chance was going past RWG and heard Margarethe playing the self-same piece. He pursued the girl, chased her up into the school clocktower and from there pushed her out of the window. When he gathered up the sheets of music, he noticed that of all the pages, the first page with the dedication was missing. As much as he searched in the schoolyard, the music room and in Margarethe's leather satchel, he couldn't find the crucial page anywhere. In his distress, he wrote a new beginning for the sonata and hoped the first page would remain lost forever.

And now we come to pure speculation. Margarethe had apparently hidden the page in the pocket of her costume skirt. But why? Did she know the significance of the dedication? Had her father let her in on the secret and had she wanted to blackmail Albert with it, since her father no longer could? Or did she hide the sheet because it could be valuable, as security in the difficult time of war? It was certainly reassuring to have an ace up your sleeve. What had really motivated Margarethe to leave the page in her costume skirt pocket while she was practising the piece we will never know. At any rate, she didn't commit suicide, we know that from the old diaries. It's a pity that there are no living relatives who would find the news a consolation."

"Well, we've solved two murders in one fell swoop and flushed out a pimp to boot. If that isn't a good result, what is? Bonsai hasn't got anything to complain about," Tabea declared, pleased.

"Okay, if there are no more questions to be answered, then we'll get back to our normal duties. Good work everybody," Doris concluded, taking this opportunity to praise everyone once more, and then stood up to end the meeting.

The other officers left the room, but Doris held Lotte back.

"Hey, is everything okay with you? Are you coming to terms with it?" she asked softly.

Lotte nodded sadly.

"I have to, don't I? He would have absolutely been the man of my dreams. That's why I wasn't objective. It could have gone really badly."

"It could have. But if you had remained completely objective, then you wouldn't have agreed to meet him. And then we wouldn't have caught him in the act. Everything happens for a reason."

"Yes, perhaps. And perhaps my mother is right with her dumb saying about other mothers."

"What other mothers?"

"Well, they have beautiful sons, too."

Lotte made a discreet nod in the direction of Andi, who was just going out the door, and who winked at Doris. She just shook her head, amused.

"Well yes, similar interests aren't bad for a relationship. Good luck and have a good time after work."

"After work? Now? It's only just turned eleven."

"I know, but haven't we earned it, don't you think?"

Lotte sprinted after the uniform officers and Doris went briefly back to her office to fetch her jacket. There was a knock on the frame of the open door and Rainer Kollrab looked back in.

"Red wine for lunch?" he asked and smiled warmly at Doris. She looked up and smiled back.

"I'd love to. But please, at room temperature."

And a few sentences in conclusion …

When the suggestion was made to me in the autumn of 2016 to join the student theatre project "Crime Scene Bayreuth – Hunt for Clues at RWG," I immediately fired up with enthusiasm and arrived at the first meeting excited and curious. It soon became clear that it would not remain just a murder mystery that was going to be staged as a play in the anniversary year, but that a book of the play was also going to appear. That was the starter's gun for many creative meetings and a never-wanting-to-end exchange of emails.

Now, months later, I have set an endpoint for my novel and I have to admit it was one of the most exciting projects that I have ever been a part of. It was not always that simple, for most of the characters were given to me beforehand, as was the plot. I found it difficult at times to slip into characters that were not 'mine', but in time they did indeed become mine. Moreover, the action taking place so long in the past, making it almost an historical crime novel, was very unusual for me. Finally, I came under deadline pressure, for in contrast to all my previous publications, towards the end I felt time implacably weighing on my back – a completely new experience for me.

Nevertheless, I am happy to have let myself be placed on these scales and only regret that our common project must now come to an end.

I am extremely happy to have been, in this unusual way, a small part of the history of RWG, a school that, incidentally, was attended just a few years after Margarethe and Lisette by my grandmother.

Heartfelt thanks go to …

Angelika Guder-Späth, who summoned me into her team, again and again encouraged me with her enthusiasm and energy and so made this book possible in the first place.

All participants in the theatre project "Crime Scene Bayreuth – Search for Clues at RWG," who gave me so many ideas, passages of text and suggestions.

Maite Schmidt and Sabrina Haugg for being eager readers.

Katharina Bouillon for her successful cover design and artwork.

Katharina Wagner, who made time for our presentations and who made some suggestions for changes.

My family, who in the final weeks lived with my night shifts and who for days on end had to walk around me on tiptoes while I sat at the kitchen table with my laptop, besieged by countless thickly printed pages, reacting most indignantly to the slightest interruption.

Antje Haugg

Dear Book Friend,

I'm happy to use this opportunity introduce myself and my books:

I was born in Bayreuth in 1965. I'm married, the mother of four children. I began writing while still at school. At first my writings were poems and lyrics for songs. Later in my school years I came to short stories, among which was a first draft of *Teufelsbraten (Devils)*.

In 1982 I won the regional lyric prize of the '*goldene Liebri*'. In 1988 I was published for the first time in the anthology *Meine Gefühle schlagen Purzelbäume (My Feelings do Somersaults)*.

After that my professional life brought about a lengthy hiatus in my writing. Only through my children did I come back to writing.

I have already published several books.

The themes are widespread:

Prinzessin Mandarina was conceived especially for beginner readers.

Auf geht's, Minitigers (Let's Go, Minitigers) deals with friendship and prejudices in an ice hockey team.

Teufelsbraten concerns first love, patchwork families and two gangs that at first are enemies but over time fight side by side and even join up to play detectives.

Sternenstaub über Bayreuth (Stardust over Bayreuth) is a romantic book about first love, guardian angels and the search for a mother who has disappeared.

The Bayreuth detective novel *Blutige Kufen (Blood Stained Skates)* is again set in the world of ice hockey. Inspector Julia Lehmann must investigate and in so doing makes the mistake of falling in love with a suspect.

Murder and music are linked in the Bayreuth detective novel *Notenspur in Moll (A Very Musical Murder)* and makes the connection between the Richard Wagner Gymnasium of 1917 and a century on.

In addition to these novels I have already written short stories on various topics for several anthologies.

Almost as important and dear to me as writing are the readings I regularly present in schools in the Bayreuth region as well as further afield. My principal object with the readings – as with the writing of my books – is to encourage reading in people who up to now have not begun with books. As a logical extension of this involvement is my participation in the Easy Reading Project of the publisher Elvea Verlag, where already *Die Teufelsbraten, Prinzessin Mandarina* as well as *Blutige Kufen* (in large print) have appeared.

Angelika Guder-Späth

Angelika Guder-Späth first saw light of day on September 13, 1960, in Herford in North Rhine-Westphalia, where she completed school at the Königen-Mathilde-Gymnasium (Queen Mathilde Grammar School) in 1979.

After studying national resources management at the Paderborn College of Higher Education in 1979/1980, she moved to the Franconia region of Bavaria where from 1980 she studied German Literature and History for Grammar School Teaching at Würzburg Teachers College. She has remained in Franconia ever since.

Following the academic side of her teacher training she worked for three years on the Historical Atlas of Bavaria, then did her practical teacher training at the Spardorf / Karlstadt Grammar School and worked at the Platen Grammar School in Ansbach up to 1994. During this time she married Hartmut Späth in 1992.

After her daughter Isabelle was born in 1994 the family moved to Emtmannsberg near Bayreuth and then moved to Eckersdorf on the western outskirts of Bayreuth in 1997. In 1999 her daughter Victoria came into the world.

From 1995 to the present day Angelika Guder-Späth has been a teacher at Richard Wagner Gymnasium in Bayreuth, where she has been the drama coordinator since 2000.

The *Notenspur in Moll* theatre project came out of the extracurricular class *Crime Scene Bayreuth – Search for Clues at RWG and* was presented as a theatre production as part of the commemorations for the anniversary of Richard Wagner Gymnasium in October 2017.

A word about the translation …

It was a parting gift from Angelika Guder-Späth that introduced me to the novel I have translated as *A Very Musical Murder* I was leaving to return to Australia after one of my regular visits to Bayreuth, where my wife, Heather, and I had the good fortune to spend a teacher exchange year in 1994. We fell in love with Bayreuth at first sight and made such good friends, notable among them Angelika Guder-Späth and her ebullient husband, Harty, that we still stay in regular contact and visit as often as we can.

1994 with Harty Späth and Angelika Guder-Späth

I was so captivated by Antje Haugg's text, a gripping crime mystery, which at the same time uncannily conveys the essence of her Bayreuth home, that I quickly felt that it should be made available to a wider audience through an English translation. With a degree in English and German literature, I said to myself, "Why don't I do it?"

Here is the fruit of my, Antje's and Angelika's labours in a new, English translation of Antje's 2017 German original. I hope you enjoy it as much as I enjoyed translating it for you.

Heather and I

Chris Ritter

**And here the accomplices from the extracurricular class
"Bayreuth Crime Scene – Hunt for Clues at RWG"**

Luisa Ermer, Alina Hägel, Charlotte Heß, Alexandra
Heyse, Lisa Kania, Maja Lowack, Klara Popp,
Lisa Prantschke, Amelie Salzborn, Alexandra Schmidt,
Valerie Sell, Dominik Tobolewski, Alina Weiß, Hanna
Ziegler, Nina Zöllner

**Unfortunately, not all the suspects can be included in
this police investigation photo.**

www.ingramcontent.com/pod-product-compliance
Lightning Source LLC
La Vergne TN
LVHW041456170726
843492LV00005B/1259